Under the Bisexual Umbrella

This book focuses on the complexities of the bisexual umbrella—the phrase that is often used to describe a wide range of sexual identities, attractions, and behaviors that indicate attraction to more than one gender. As a consequence, the bisexual umbrella groups together a very heterogeneous group of people. The writers in this book each grapple with how the bisexual umbrella is applied to a variety of communities, people, and experiences, and discuss the benefits and costs of these applications. Topics include exploration of the similarities and differences between two-spirit people and bisexuals, including how their health concerns overlap and diverge; detailing of personal and empirical experiences of sexual fluidity; descriptions of how bisexual, pansexual, and queer people conceptualize sexual identity; and explorations of pansexuality. Through these writings, the diversity underneath the bisexual umbrella is revealed.

The chapters in this book were originally published as a special issue of the *Journal of Bisexuality*.

Corey E. Flanders is an Assistant Professor in the Department of Psychology and Education at Mount Holyoke University, South Hadley, MA, USA. Her research and teaching interests focus on issues of identity and health equity as they relate to the experiences of queer and trans people broadly, and bisexual people in particular.

Under the Bisexual Umbrella

Diversity of Identity and Experience

Edited by
Corey E. Flanders

Routledge
Taylor & Francis Group
LONDON AND NEW YORK

First published 2019
by Routledge
2 Park Square, Milton Park, Abingdon, Oxon, OX14 4RN, UK

and by Routledge
711 Third Avenue, New York, NY 10017, USA

Routledge is an imprint of the Taylor & Francis Group, an informa business

British Library Cataloguing-in-Publication Data
A catalogue record for this book is available from the British Library

ISBN13: 978-1-138-33087-0

Typeset in Minion Pro
by codeMantra

Publisher's Note
The publisher accepts responsibility for any inconsistencies that may have arisen during the conversion of this book from journal articles to book chapters, namely the possible inclusion of journal terminology.

Disclaimer
Every effort has been made to contact copyright holders for their permission to reprint material in this book. The publishers would be grateful to hear from any copyright holder who is not here acknowledged and will undertake to rectify any errors or omissions in future editions of this book.

Contents

Citation Information

The chapters in this book were originally published in the *Journal of Bisexuality*, volume 17, issue 1 (March 2017). When citing this material, please use the original page numbering for each article, as follows:

Introduction
Under the Bisexual Umbrella: Diversity of Identity and Experience
Corey E. Flanders
Journal of Bisexuality, volume 17, issue 1 (March 2017) pp. 1–6

Chapter 1
Two-Spirit and Bisexual People: Different Umbrella, Same Rain
Margaret Robinson
Journal of Bisexuality, volume 17, issue 1 (March 2017) pp. 7–29

Chapter 2
Home-o: Being at Home with Reflections on Hetero-Homosexual Identity
Joshua Nash
Journal of Bisexuality, volume 17, issue 1 (March 2017) pp. 30–38

Chapter 3
Defining Bisexuality: Young Bisexual and Pansexual People's Voices
Corey E. Flanders, Marianne E. LeBreton, Margaret Robinson, Jing Bian, and Jaime Alonso Caravaca-Morera
Journal of Bisexuality, volume 17, issue 1 (March 2017) pp. 39–57

Chapter 4
What's in a Name? Exploring Pansexuality Online
Christopher K. Belous and Melissa L. Bauman
Journal of Bisexuality, volume 17, issue 1 (March 2017) pp. 58–72

Chapter 5
Perceptions of Individuals Who Are Non-monosexuals held by Graduate Students: A Q Methodological Study
Colton Brown, Diane Montgomery, and Tonya R. Hammer
Journal of Bisexuality, volume 17, issue 1 (March 2017) pp. 73–87

Chapter 6

"It's not Pans, It's People": Student and Teacher Perspectives on Bisexuality and Pansexuality
Alicia Anne Lapointe
Journal of Bisexuality, volume 17, issue 1 (March 2017) pp. 88–107

Chapter 7

"Regardless of Their Gender": Descriptions of Sexual Identity among Bisexual, Pansexual, and Queer Identified Individuals
M. Paz Galupo, Johanna L. Ramirez, and Lex Pulice-Farrow
Journal of Bisexuality, volume 17, issue 1 (March 2017) pp. 108–124

Chapter 8

We're Here and We're Queer: Sexual Orientation and Sexual Fluidity Differences Between Bisexual and Queer Women
Ethan H. Mereish, Sabra L. Katz-Wise, and Julie Woulfe
Journal of Bisexuality, volume 17, issue 1 (March 2017) pp. 125–139

Notes on Contributors

Melissa L. Bauman has worked professionally developing public policy briefings for legislatures related to underserved populations and completing research on marginalized populations. She has a background in social services and nonprofit agencies for rural and underserved populations with mental illness. She currently works for the Department of Juvenile Justice, Washington, DC, USA, providing mental health services to adolescent inmates.

Christopher K. Belous is an Assistant Professor in the Department of Psychiatry and Behavioral Sciences' Master of Family Therapy Program on the Atlanta/Piedmont Campus of Mercer University School of Medicine, USA, where he also serves as the Clinic Director for the on-site graduate training facility. His research focuses on sex and sexuality—broadly defined, social justice and couple and family therapy education and supervision.

Jing Bian is an Undergraduate Student at the University of Toronto, Canada. She is currently volunteering with the Re:searching for LGBTQ Health Team at the Centre for Addiction and Mental Health.

Colton Brown is a Doctoral Candidate in the Counseling Psychology program at Oklahoma State University, Stillwater, OK, USA. His research primarily consists of work with the bi/pan/queer/fluidC community, the use of media in counseling, and foster and adoptive care. He is the Coordinator of Programming for the bi/pan/queer/fulidC community at the Dennis R. Neill Equality Center in Tulsa, Oklahoma.

Jaime Alonso Caravaca-Morera is a Nurse and Professor of the Clinical Simulation Center at the University of Costa Rica, San Pedro Montes de Oca, Costa Rica. He is also a Doctoral Student of the Post-Graduate Nursing Program at the Federal University of Santa Catarina, Brazil.

Corey E. Flanders is an Assistant Professor in the Department of Psychology and Education at Mount Holyoke University, South Hadley, MA, USA. Her research and teaching interests focus on issues of identity and health equity as they relate to the experiences of queer and trans people broadly, and bisexual people in particular.

M. Paz Galupo is Professor of Psychology and Director of the Sexual and Gender Identity Research lab at Towson University, USA. Paz's research interests focus on understanding the intersection of sexual orientation and gender identity as they are negotiated in the context of social and personal relationships, with a particular focus on bisexual/plurisexual and transgender experience.

Tonya R. Hammer is an Assistant Professor in the Counseling and Counseling Psychology program at Oklahoma State University, Stillwater, OK, USA. Her research primarily focuses on relational-cultural theory, LGBTQC issues, and creativity in counseling. She is the President for the Association for Lesbian, Gay, Bisexual, and Transgender Issues in Counseling within the American Counseling Association.

Sabra L. Katz-Wise is an Assistant Professor at the Department of Pediatrics, Harvard Medical School, Boston, MA, USA, and a Research Scientist at the Division of Adolescent/Young Adult Medicine at Boston Children's Hospital, USA.

Alicia Anne Lapointe is a Research Associate who researches Gay-Straight Alliances (GSA) and student activism in public and Catholic schools in Ontario, Canada. Alicia also created and instructs the undergraduate course Lesbian, Gay, Bisexual, Trans_, Two-Spirit, Queer/Questioning (LGBT2Q) Issues in Education (2014–present).

Marianne E. LeBreton started working for the Coping and Resilience (CORE) Research Team at McGill University, Montreal, QC, Canada, in 2012, where she is the Project Coordinator for the Canadian Institutes of Health Research (CIHR)-funded project "Bisexual Identity: Implications for the Mental and Sexual Health of Men". She is a Sexologist whose work focuses on gender identity and sexual orientation. Her current research focuses on bisexuality.

Ethan H. Mereish is an Assistant Professor in the Department of Health Studies at American University, Washington, DC, USA. He was a Postdoctoral Research Fellow at the Center for Alcohol and Addiction Studies and the Department of Behavioral and Social Sciences at Brown University, Providence, RI, USA.

Diane Montgomery is a Regents Professor in the School of Applied Health and Educational Psychology at Oklahoma State University, Stillwater, OK, USA. Her works primarily consists of Q methodological research in the realm of education. She previously served as the President of the Society for the Scientific Study of Subjectivity and has consulted for systemic change with local schools.

Joshua Nash is an Associate Professor at Aarhus University in Denmark. His research intersects ethnography, the anthropology of religion, architecture, pilgrimage studies, and language documentation. He has conducted linguistic fieldwork on Norfolk Island, Pitcairn Island, and Kangaroo Island; environmental and ethnographic fieldwork in Vrindavan, India; and architectural research in outback Australia.

Lex Pulice-Farrow is a Clinical Psychology Graduate Student at Towson University, USA. Lex's research interests center on sexual orientation and gender identity, with a focus on transgender and gender nonconforming individuals.

Johanna L. Ramirez is a Clinical Psychology Graduate Student at Towson University, USA. Johanna's research interests focus on the intersection of sexual and racial identity, with a particular focus on LGBT people of color.

Margaret Robinson is currently an Assistant Professor in Indigenous Studies in the Sociology & Social Anthropology department at Dalhousie University, Halifax, NS, Canada, and an Affiliate Research Scientist at the Centre for Addiction & Mental Health in Toronto, ON, Canada. Her research work examines mental health and substance use in Indigenous and Settler populations, especially among sexual and gender minority people.

Julie Woulfe is a Clinical Fellow at the Department of Psychiatry at Harvard Medical School, Boston, MA, USA, and a Graduate Student at the Department of Counseling, Developmental, and Educational Psychology at Boston College, USA.

INTRODUCTION TO THE SPECIAL ISSUE

Under the Bisexual Umbrella: Diversity of Identity and Experience

Corey E. Flanders

I am pleased to introduce the special issue, "Under the Bisexual Umbrella: Diversity of Identity and Experience." Included in this issue is a series of articles detailing many complexities within the bisexual umbrella. These complexities range from different perspectives on defining and choosing identity labels, to exploration of personal sexualities, to exploring implications of what being under the umbrella might mean for nonbisexual identities. In this introduction, I first provide a description of the bisexual umbrella, discuss how community members and researchers use it, and then delve further into the intricacies of the concept as detailed by many of the authors.

Bisexual umbrella coverage

The 'bisexual umbrella' is a phrase that is most commonly used to describe a range of nonmonosexual identities, behaviors, and forms of attraction. Although this includes people who identify as bisexual, it has also been used to group together bisexuality with other nonmonosexual identities, notably pansexual, queer, and fluid as discussed by many of the authors in this special issue. As Robinson writes in "Two-Spirit and Bisexual People: Different Umbrella, Same Rain," two-spirit identity is also often brought under the umbrella. Beyond nonmonosexual identities, the umbrella is sometimes used to cover people who do not identify with a nonmonosexual identity but engage in behaviors or experience attraction to more than one gender, an experience explored by Nash in "Home-o: Being at Home with Reflections on Hetero-Homosexual Identity," as well as purported by participants in Flanders, LeBreton, Robinson, Bian, and Caravaca-Morera (2017), "Defining Bisexuality: Young Bisexual and Pansexual People's Voices." For some people who are included under the bisexual umbrella, it provides welcome cover and a metaphorical gathering place for a community that often feels it does not belong anywhere. For others, it may feel inappropriately applied and like an attempt to promote homogeneity where there is, in fact, anything but. There, too, are implications for researchers who choose to conceptualize bisexuality and nonmonosexuality at its broadest and most inclusive, or to create more selective inclusion criteria in their research.

One challenge of uniting nonmonosexual communities is the balancing act of being inclusive enough to avoid unintentionally excluding others, while remaining cohesive enough to move together in collective action. The bisexual umbrella serves in this purpose as a grouping device for an incredibly diverse set of individuals; some of those who are included choose to be grouped together, and for others, the choice is made for them by researchers or society at large. A step in recognizing the complexity under the bisexual umbrella is to understand that some people select bisexual and/or other nonmonosexual identities and also explicitly identify under the bisexual umbrella. Others who identify as nonmonosexual do not identify under the bisexual umbrella or only do so in certain social contexts.

Researchers and society further complicate the bisexual umbrella inclusion/exclusion criteria in ways that may have very little to do with the agency of nonmonosexual people themselves. For example, some people may find identities such as pansexuality unintelligible, potentially due to and pan erasure, as discussed in Belous and Bauman's, "What's in a Name? Exploring Pansexuality Online." In this case, pansexual people may be misidentified and grouped under the bisexual umbrella, regardless of whether they actually identify with the umbrella. In other examples, researchers may have a question that is applicable to all people who engage in sexual behavior with more than one gender (creating an expansive umbrella) whereas others may have questions specific to people who identify as bisexual and queer (creating a restrictive umbrella). The bisexual umbrella then is not a static, unchanging façade, but rather a shape-shifting construct, expanding, and constricting depending upon a variety of factors that push and pull against one another.

Bisexual umbrella benefits

If there are tensions, what are the benefits of the bisexual umbrella? First, as noted above, there are many similarities and shared experiences across disparate groups under the bisexual umbrella. One overarching issue that unites the largest number of nonmonosexual people is the monosexist culture that we exist in, that privileges and reinforces relationships and attractions to only one gender, neatly conforming to a binary system of sexuality and attraction. Brown, Montgomery, and Hammer address how perceptions held by graduate students can affect all non-monosexual people, regardless of specific identity, in "Perceptions of Individuals Who Are Non-monosexuals held by Graduate Students: A Q Methodological Study." As noted by Lapointe in "'It's not Pans, It's People': Student and Teacher Perspectives on Bisexuality and Pansexuality," though the youth interviewed in Gay Straight Alliances (GSAs) do not see pansexuality and bisexuality as interchangeable, they recognize the need for space to discuss and explore and be bisexual and/or pansexual. Further, Galupo, Ramirez, and Pulice-Farrow, state in their article, "'Regardless of their Gender': Descriptions of Sexual Identity among Bisexual, Pansexual, and Queer Identified Individuals," that there are more similarities than differences in the way bisexual, pansexual, and queer people conceptualize their identities. In these cases, it potentially makes sense for our different subcommunities under the umbrella to band together and advocate for recognition and inclusion of non-monosexual people. The finding that so many of us simultaneously embody multiple umbrella identities, such as bisexual *and* queer, further supports this union (Mitchell, Davis, & Galupo, 2015).

Second, as indicated by Mereish, Katz-Wise, and Woulfe in, "We're Here and We're Queer: Sexual Orientation and Sexual Fluidity Differences between Bisexual and Queer Women," as well as Robinson, one area of similarity is level of income and experience of poverty between bisexual and queer women, as well as between bisexual people and two-spirit people. Research has consistently identified higher levels of poverty among bisexual and other non-monosexual groups in contrast to their monosexual peers (Gorman, Denney, Dowdy, & Medeiros, 2015; Ross et al., 2016). Poverty and income inequality may then be considered a social justice issue for individuals under the umbrella, and the greater number of people advocating for income equality, the more likely our voices are to be heard.

Another uniting factor among the wide range of people included under the umbrella is the higher vulnerability for negative health outcomes (Schick & Dodge, 2012), which is also related to income inequality (Braveman, Egerter, & Williams, 2011; Ross et al., 2016). Whether nonmonosexuality is categorized by identity or behavior, researchers consistently report higher rates of negative mental and physical health outcomes among nonmonosexual people in contrast to our monosexual peers, though how nonmonosexuality is conceptualized within research affects the overall outcomes (Bauer & Brennan, 2013). Like with income inequality, the umbrella in this case may provide a platform for a critical mass of nonmonosexual people to advocate for health policy makers, researchers, and health care service providers to consider the specific needs of non-monosexual people.

Bisexual umbrella costs

On the other hand, if there are tensions underneath the umbrella, what are the differences between groups, and what are the costs of ignoring these differences in favor of highlighting the umbrella, or the things we have in common? One area of difference, as noted by Lapointe, as well as Galupo and colleagues, is how non-monosexual people define their sexual identities, and how that differs between groups. One of the more contentious issues in this area is the insistence that bisexuality reinforces a gender binary, whereas other identities (i.e., queer and pansexual) facilitate openness to more genders beyond the binary. The complicated thing here is that rarely do people agree upon how to define or embody a single identity, much less an umbrella identity. The articles by Flanders et al. and Galupo et al. note that though many people who identify as bisexual use binary language to describe their sexuality, many also do not. Bisexual activists have been resisting the insistence that bisexuality is inherently binary for decades. The Bisexual Manifesto (Bay Area Bisexual Network, 1990), published in *Anything that Moves*, resisted the conceptualization of bisexuality as binary. The major bisexual advocacy groups do not define 'bisexuality' in binary terms. Yet the message persists. In part, this may be due to the fact that some people identify as bisexual and are only attracted to two genders. Sometimes this may be cisgender men and women, but other times it may mean cisgender women and nonbinary people. And in part, the persistence of this message may be due to people who do not identify as bisexual continuing to insist that bisexuality always and necessarily means binary attraction, erasing the experiences of many bisexual people.

Ultimately, using a bisexual umbrella is complicated because we have umbrellas within umbrellas within umbrellas. Bisexuality as a single identity encompasses so many different meanings and attractions and behaviors for people who explicitly identify as bisexual. The general identity definition most commonly used, attraction to more than one gender, then leaves room for the multitudinous expressions of that identity. And, the umbrella covers people who explicitly do not identify as bisexual but elect to be considered under the umbrella; and the umbrella is held over other individuals whose behaviors or attractions may align with the umbrella, but they do not consider themselves as a part of this group. People under the umbrella are also more likely to identify with more than one sexual identity label (Mitchell et al., 2015). Further, people under the umbrella embody so many other identities beyond sexuality, including but not limited to race, gender, ability, religion, and class, that affect their experience and equitable inclusion under the umbrella.

At the crux of these tensions is the erasure of diversity under the bisexual umbrella. It simultaneously serves as a way to create community space and to obscure the beautiful and important variances that occur within nonmonosexual communities. At its most expansive, the umbrella may enable social advocacy that would be more difficult without it, but at what cost? Do we run the risk of perpetuating similar forms of erasure underneath the umbrella that non-monosexual people experience in society generally? If so, would that form of erasure have similar health implications? Is it time to reconceptualize how we label the umbrella, and if so, can the reconceptualization be done in a way that does not undermine the visibility of non-monosexual identities and the decades of advocacy work by bisexual and other non-monosexual activists to have bisexuality recognized?

Concluding thoughts

There are many other words that we use to describe what I have been referring to as the "bisexual umbrella" and non-monosexuality. Some resist the term non-monosexuality as it defines a population by what it is not (i.e., monosexual) and prefer other identity terms that are inclusive of attraction to more than one gender, such as plurisexual (Mitchell et al., 2015), polysexual (Hutchins & Williams, 2012), pomosexual (Queen & Schimel, 1997), and multisexual. Others prefer the label of queer, though this term is problematic as an umbrella term in that it does not specify the existence of attraction to multiple genders. Given the diversity of identity and experience under the umbrella, perhaps adopting one of these other terms as an umbrella term would alleviate the tension that occurs with the constant shape shifting of the umbrella. Bisexual, pansexual, queer, fluid, and the many other identity groups could exist as they are without stretching or retracting to (un)cover others, but we could still benefit from coming together for collective action. This would certainly mean that for groups who are marginalized in the umbrella communities, such as two-spirit people, there needs to be a specific focus to let people "opt-in" as opposed to be forcefully covered. Further, as recommended by intersectional theorists (Bowleg, 2012), collective action priorities should be determined by those who experience multiple forms of marginalization to not erase the needs and experiences of Indigenous people, communities of color, people with disabilities, or people living in poverty that are a part of the community.

As an individual and a researcher, I do not know what the best answer is to accommodate these competing advantages and disadvantages of the umbrella. As an individual, I desire to live in a world in which all identities are equally respected and are given equitable space to exist, without being misidentified or erased. As a researcher, I desire to conduct meaningful work that serves to benefit as many people under the umbrella as possible. The authors in this special issue make substantial contributions to the community and intellectual conversations supporting these desires, and these contributions will hopefully further inspire the continuing conversation within and beyond our umbrella communities.

References

Bauer, G. R., & Brennan, D. J. (2013). The problem with 'behavioral bisexuality': Assessing sexual orientation in survey research. *Journal of Bisexuality, 13*(2), 148–165. doi:10.1080/15299716.2013.782260

Bay Area Bisexual Network. (1990). The bisexual manifesto. Anything that moves.

Belous, C. K., & Bauman, M. L. (2017). What's in a name? Exploring pansexuality online. *Journal of Bisexuality, 17*(1), 58–72. doi:10.1080/15299716.2016.1224212

Bowleg, L. (2012). The problem with the phrase women and minorities: intersectionality-an important framework for public health. *American Journal of Public Health, 102*(7), 1267–1273.

Braveman, P., Egerter, S., & Williams, D. R. (2011). The social determinants of health: coming of age. *Annual Review of Public Health, 32*, 381–398. doi:10.1146/annurev-publhealth-031210-101218

Brown, C., Montgomery, D., & Hammer, T.R. (2017). Perceptions held by graduate students of non-monosexuals: A Q methodological study. *Journal of Bisexuality, 17*(1), 73–87.

Flanders, C. E., LeBreton, M. E., Robinson, M., Bian, J., & Caravaca-Morera, J. A. (2017). Defining bisexuality: Young bisexual and pansexual people's voices. *Journal of Bisexuality, 17*(1), 39–57. doi:10.1080/15299716.2016.1227016

Galupo, M. P., Ramirez, J. L., & Pulice-Farrow, L. (2017). "Regardless of their gender": Descriptions of sexual identity among bisexual, pansexual, and queer identified individuals. *Journal of Bisexuality, 17*(1), 108–124. doi:10.1080/15299716.2016.1228491

Gorman, B. K., Denney, J. T., Dowdy, H., & Medeiros, R. A. (2015). A new piece of the puzzle: Sexual orientation, gender, and physical health status. *Demography, 52,* 1357–1382. doi:10.1007/s13524-015-0406-1

Hutchins, L., & Williams, H. (2012). *Sexuality, religion, and the sacred: Bisexual, pansexual and polysexual perspectives.* New York, NY: Routledge.

Lapointe, A. A. (2017). "It's not pans, it's people": Student and teacher perspectives on bisexuality and pansexuality. *Journal of Bisexuality, 17*(1), 88–107. doi:10.1080/15299716.2016.1196157

Mereish, E. H., Katz-Wise, S. L., & Woulfe, J. (2017). We're here and we're queer: Sexual orientation and sexual fluidity differences between bisexual and queer women. *Journal of Bisexuality, 17*(1), 125–139. doi:10.1080/15299716.2016.1217448

Mitchell, R. C., Davis, K. S., & Galupo, M. P. (2015). Comparing perceived experiences of prejudice among self-identified plurisexual individuals. *Psychology & Sexuality,* 6(3), 245–257. doi:10.1080/19419899.2014.940372

Nash, J. (2017). Home-o: Being at home with reflections on hetero-homosexual identity. *Journal of Bisexuality, 17*(1), 30–38. doi:10.1080/15299716.2016.1220341

Queen, C., & Schimel, L. (1997). *PoMosexuals: Challenging assumptions about gender and sexuality.* San Francisco, CA: Cleis Press Inc.

Robinson, M. (2017). Two-spirit and bisexual people: different umbrella, same rain. *Journal of Bisexuality, 17*(1), 7–29. doi:10.1080/15299716.2016.1261266

Ross, L. E., O'Gorman, L., MacLeod, M. A., Bauer, G. R., MacKay, J., & Robinson, M. (2016). Bisexuality, poverty and mental health: A mixed methods analysis. *Social Science & Medicine, 156,* 64–72. doi:10.1016/j.socscimed.2016.03.009

Schick, V., & Dodge, B. (2012). Introduction to the special issue: Bisexual health: Unpacking the paradox. *Journal of Bisexuality, 12*(2), 161–167. doi:10.1080/15299716.2012.674849

Two-Spirit and Bisexual People: Different Umbrella, Same Rain

Margaret Robinson

ABSTRACT
Increasingly, two-spirit identity is being included as one of the identities under the bisexual umbrella, yet there has been very little discussion about how this inclusion might affect two-spirit people, the research that pertains to us, or the services shaped by such data. This article draws upon personal experience as a two-spirit and bisexual woman as well as upon research conducted with two-spirit people in the province of Ontario, Canada. Five points of comparison between bisexual and two-spirit identity are examined: (1) the complexity of our identities, (2) the role of spirituality, (3) our elevated rates of poverty, (4) sexual violence, and (5) the influence of colonialism. Although bisexual and two-spirit identities share a number of commonalities they have key differences in cultural context and meaning.

I am an Indigenous scholar and health researcher who identifies as two-spirit and bisexual. In Canada, where I live, it is increasingly common to include two-spirit identity in research pertaining to bisexuality. Yet I must ask: What similarities exist between bisexuality and two-spirit identity? Are they strong enough to justify including two-spirit participants under the bisexual umbrella? What how might such inclusion affect data analysis?

This article draws on my lived experience as well as on my recent community-based research (CBR) with bisexual and two-spirit people. Although the term 'Indigenous' has emerged as a preferred collective self-identity, the majority of research involving Indigenous people often identifies us using the labels preferred by Settler governments. In Canada, for example, 'Aboriginal' is a category with a specific legal meaning defined in Section 35(2)a of the Constitution Act (1982) and refers collectively to three distinct Indigenous groups: The First Nations, the Métis, and the Inuit. When reporting research data gathered from Indigenous populations I use the terms under which the information was collected. I begin by outlining use of the bisexual umbrella within health research, and the concept of two-spirit identity, then describe the data sets I use and my analytical approach to explore five points of comparison between bisexual and two-spirit identity.

Bisexuality and the bisexual umbrella within health research

Bisexuality has a history of being used to describe physical sexual characteristics and the gender expressions that were associated with sex at the time. Researchers Richard von Krafft-Ebing and Henry Havelock Ellis initially named bisexuality "psychosexual hermaphrodism" (Storr, 2013), viewing attraction to women and men to be the result of a brain that was masculine and feminine. Similarly, Sigmund Freud and Wilhelm Fleiss believed the human fetus was male and female in early stages and viewed same-sex attraction as an expression of incomplete psychological sex development (Garber, 1995; Greenberg, 1990). Eventually scientists began to use "bisexual" to refer exclusively to sexuality and used the now outdated term "hermaphrodite", and later "intersex", to refer to physical sex characteristics. However, the idea that sexuality is a reflection of sex-based brain characteristics is still current in some research (LeVay, 2010).

Within health research today, bisexual often becomes a catch-all category for those who do not identify as straight, gay, or lesbian. Shiri Eisner's (2011) infographic, The Bisexual Umbrella, includes identities such as pansexuality, omnisexual, polysexual, queer, fluid, homo- and hetero-flexible, and bi-curious. There is some logic for recoding these identities as bisexual, such as their shared exposure to biphobia and monosexism. As well, many bisexual people hold multiple identities including pansexual, queer, or fluid (Barker, Richards, Jones, Bowes-Catton, & Plowman, 2012), making it difficult to frame other plurisexual identities as distinct from bisexuality. Popular distinctions, such as the stereotype that bisexuals hold a binary view of gender while pansexuals do not, is not borne out by recent research (Flanders, LeBreton, Robinson, Bian, & Caravaca-Morea, in press; Galupo, Ramirez, & Pulice-Farrow, in press). However, use of the bisexual umbrella may obscure differences within plurisexual populations. A study by Mitchell, Davis, and Galupo (2015), for example, found that individuals who were bisexuals reported experiencing more hostility from gay and lesbian peers than did participants who were pansexual, queer, or fluid participants. Another recent study found that participants whose only reported identity was bisexual (as opposed to bisexual in addition to something else) were most likely to have multiple negative health outcomes such as depression, anxiety, suicide ideation, problematic alcohol use, or the use of multiple substances (Bauer, Flanders, MacLeod, & Ross, 2016). By comparison, those who identified as something other than bisexual (e.g., pansexual but not bisexual) were two thirds as likely as bisexual-only participants to have multiple outcomes, and participants who reported having identities in addition to bisexual (e.g., bisexual and pansexual) were one third as likely to report multiple negative health outcomes (Bauer et al., 2016). Such studies highlight that those of us under the bisexual umbrella may have significantly different experiences and may be affected differently by stressors (Barker et al., 2012; Galupo, Mitchell, & Davis, 2015; Mitchell et al, 2015).

Two-spirit identity

Two-spirit, a translation of the Ojibwe term *niizh manidoowag*, is an identity that emerged in 1990 to describe third or fourth gender people in Indigenous cultures (e.g., First Nations, Métis, Inuit, American Indian, and Alaskan Native) across what is now called North America. As two-spirit scholar Harlan Pruden notes, the historical phenomena is not a sexual identity. "Two-spirit within a traditional or pre-contact setting is a gender," Pruden states. "Gender dictates your role within the society. Women gathered, men hunted, and us, as two-spirit people, we did a unique thing" (CBC News, 2015). A number of scholars note that people who are two-spirit performed distinctive roles in Indigenous communities such as bestowing sacred names, or serving as leaders, intermediaries, or medicine people (Garret & Barrett, 2003; Blackwood, 1997; Bullough, 1976; R. M. Carpenter, 2011; Gunn Allen, 1989; Robertson, 1997). In some cases two-spirit men joined women in preparing food and making pottery or baskets, while two-spirit women hunted and engaged in warfare (Blackwood, 1997; Cromwell, 1997).

In contemporary practice, two-spirit refers to Indigenous people whose sexual and/or gender identity is different from others. While not all Indigenous sexual or gender minority people identify as two-spirit, the label connects people across Indigenous nations and offers a common name for what were distinct identities or even distinct systems of sexuality. As J. Andrew Baker (2014) explains:

> … it became a term that people from multiple nations could identify with … and it meant that there could be a sense of belonging.… So that someone who was Aboriginal, who was LGBTQ and was being excluded could say. "I'm two spirit." and they could have a place. And they would have a group of people who they could identify with, who had similar journeys, similar stories.

While providing a common identity, terms such as two-spirit risk overwriting the sexual and gender roles that are unique to specific Indigenous nations, increasing the erasure of Indigenous cultures (Lang, 1998; Robinson, 2012, 2014a). To counter this erasure some two-spirit people also identify with terms from our Indigenous languages, such as the Anishinaabe terms *agokwe* (describing a man who is also a woman) or *agokwe-nini* (describing a woman who is also a man).

Two-spirit identity shares a number of similarities with bisexuality, but is different in ways that preclude uncritical use of the bisexual umbrella in research or health services. Two-spirit people may be included under the bisexual umbrella—perhaps because they also identity as bisexual, because they fit the criteria for a study on bisexual health, or because they experience biphobia and related oppressions—but such inclusion must not come at the expense of erasing them as Indigenous, or of overwriting their Indigenous identities as if their bisexuality is a more authentic category.

Data sets and analytical approach

My analysis draws on my experience as a two-spirit person, doing insider research, listening to two-spirit people, and learning from my community. It draws also on my experience as a bisexual woman, doing insider research, contextualizing population-based data with knowledge drawn from my own lived experience as well as that of the bisexual communities in Ontario.

My epistemological approach is *Etuaptmumk*, or two-eyed seeing, developed by Mi'kmaw Elder Albert Marshall (Hatcher, Bartlett, Marshall, & Marshall, 2009; Institute for Integrative Science & Health, 2012), in which Indigenous and Western epistemologies operate in tandem without overwriting one another. In this way, two-eyed seeing reflects the Two Row Wampum Treaty of 1613 between the Haudenosaunee and the Dutch, where two rows of purple beads represent parallel vessels travelling together (McGregor, 2008). The present uses Western traditions of critical textual hermeneutics emerging from queer, bisexual, feminist, and other critical theories, and Indigenous traditions of cultural ceremony, narrative, and the critical theoretical work of two-spirit people and Indigenous feminists. I enact two-eyed seeing within a framework of CBR. The studies on which I draw embodied CBR principles to varying degrees, but both included elements of shared decision making and ownership, bi-directional research capacity development and colearning, and the mutually beneficial creation and dissemination of knowledge (Castleden, Garvin, Huu-ay-aht First Nation., 2008; Castleden, Morgan, & Lamb, 2012; Israel, Eng, Schultz, & Parker, 2005). By bringing multiple viewpoints to bear on the data sets I aimed to achieve a three-dimensional perspective on the relationship between two-spirit and bisexual identities.

The risk & resilience study of bisexual mental health

I draw on data collected as part of Risk & Resilience, a large community-based study of bisexual mental health in Ontario, Canada, for which I was project coordinator. The research team was made up of bisexual, pansexual, and fluid identified as well as monosexual allies. Survey questions were developed in consultation with a Bisexual Community Advisory Committee of 11 people from across the province who are affiliated (to varying degrees) with bisexual identity. Members of the Committee helped determine the survey contents, led study recruitment, assisted in analyzing the data and contextualizing the findings, and some coauthored manuscripts.

This study used respondent-driven sampling to recruit people to complete an online survey. Eligibility included being attracted to more than one sex/gender, being age 16 or older, and living or receiving health services in the province of Ontario. Participants received an e-mail link by which they accessed the survey and upon completion were able to invite up to 10 peers to participate. Participants were compensated $20 for completing the survey and an additional $5 for each successful recruit. A video was produced to explain the study, introduce the researchers and our motivations, and encourage people to complete the study if invited to do so (Centre for Addiction and Mental Health, 2012). Overall, 405 people participated in the study; the present analysis draws upon data from the 38 participants who identified as Aboriginal (i.e., First Nations, Inuit, or Métis). Participant demographics are shown in Table 1.

Participants in Risk & Resilience were asked about their personal demographics, social circumstances, and mental health. Details about the measures used have been described elsewhere (MacLeod, Bauer, Ross, Robinson, & MacKay, 2015; Robinson, Sanches, & MacLeod, 2016; Ross et al., 2014; Ross et al., 2016). In addition to gathering quantitative data the survey asked a number of open-ended questions, including "What things do you like about being bisexual," and "Is there anything you would like to share about your experience of overlapping identity or oppression?" Direct quotes for the present work are drawn from these responses,

Table 1. Participant demographics.

	Risk & Resilience		Two-Spirit Roundtable	
	n	%	*n*	%
Participants	38		21	
Age range	22–57	100.00	31–67	100.00
20–29	19	51.35	1	4.76
30–39	10	27.02	4	19.04
40–49	3	8.10	10	47.61
50+	5	13.51	4	19.04
Median age	29	—	46	—
Indigenous identity[a]				
Aboriginal	38	100	—	—
First Nations	—	—	14	66.66
Inuit	—	—	2	9.52
Métis	—	—	5	23.80
Sexuality[b]				
Ambisexual	1	2.63	—	—
Biaffectionate	3	7.89	—	—
Bisensual	6	15.79	—	—
Bisexual	25	65.79	4	19.04
Fluid	8	21.05	—	—
Gay	—	—	4	19.04
Heteroflexible	3	7.89	—	—
Homoflexible	4	10.53	—	—
Omnisexual	2	5.26	—	—
Pansexual	15	39.47	—	—
Queer	18	47.37	1	4.76
Two-spirit	15	39.47	9	42.85
Other	3	7.89	3	14.28
Gender[b]				
Agokwe-nini	—	—	1	4.76
Bigender	4	10.53	—	—
Crossdresser	1	2.63	—	—
Genderqueer	9	23.68	2	9.52
Men (trans inclusive)	9	23.68	5	23.80
Two-spirit	11	28.95	9	42.85
Women (trans inclusive)	24	63.16	3	14.28
Other	5	13.15	1	4.76

[a]Participants in Risk & Resilience were asked only if they identified as Aboriginal.
[b]Questions were "choose all that apply," so results total more than 100%.

with participants' sexual and gender identities included in parentheses. Meetings with Indigenous members of the steering committee determined which quantitative variables were of interest for an analysis of the Aboriginal participant data, and a student who was attached to the project conducted the analyses. Early drafts of the results were shared with the Indigenous members of the Bisexual Community Advisory Committee, and with members of Indigenous communities in Toronto, and feedback was incorporated (Robinson, Plante, MacLeod, Cruz, & Banji, 2016).

Community driven and led research that is accountable to Indigenous communities is a response to the long history of alienating and exploitive research that Indigenous communities have endured. Risk & Resilience was a community-based research project in terms of its emergence within and involvement of the bisexual communities in Ontario, but it was less so in relation to Indigenous communities. Although two members of the advisory committee (one Elder and one younger activist) identified as two-spirit, as did the project coordinator, problems emerged around understandings of sexuality and gender, and around the marginalization of Indigeneity within the project more generally. This experience clarified the need for research grounded in an Indigenous epistemology and focused on two-spirit experience, which led directly to the development of the Two-Spirit Roundtable Project.

Two-spirit roundtable project

I was the principal investigator on the Two-Spirit Roundtable Project, a community-based study led by two-spirit people ourselves and guided by two-spirit and Indigenous ally elders and knowledge keepers. We recruited 21 two-spirit participants in two Ontario cities using online flyers and social networks and collected qualitative data using talking circles and private interviews. Eligible participants self-identified as Aboriginal and as two-spirited, or as lesbian, gay, bisexual, trans, or a related sexual identity. Participants were compensated $40 and talking circles were provided with food. Participant demographics are available in Table 1.

Research questions for this study included: (1) How do two-spirit people understand their two-spirit identity? and (2) How do two-spirit people understand and support their own mental health? Data were gathered using the conversation method, an Indigenous interview technique rooted in storytelling and relational knowing (Kovach, 2010). Participants were asked questions about their identity (e.g., "What does two-spirited mean to you?"), mental health ("e.g., What about mental health? What does that mean to you?"), coping mechanism (e.g., "What kind of things do you do for yourself when stuff gets stressful?"). Participants were also asked an open-ended question about mental health, "Is there anything you feel like we need to take into account to understand mental health and two-spirited people?" Direct quotes from this study are drawn from answers to these questions, with the speaker's sexual and gender identities included in parentheses.

Interviews and talking circles were transcribed verbatim, and deidentified. Textual analysis was secondary to analysis of the audio recording. I listened to recordings multiple times, revisiting the experience in my head and heart, as I reread the transcripts. Responses were coded according to the Anishinaabe Medicine Wheel, whose four quadrants represent physical, emotional, mental, and spiritual health. This framework was chosen because it reflected the cultural framework of many of the participants, and because participants repeatedly evoked the Medicine Wheel as significant during their interviews.

Data analysis

The present analysis draws on data from these and other studies, as well as my lived experience as a two-spirit woman, to focus on five points of comparison between bisexual and two-spirit people. These points are (1) the complex nature of our identities, (2) the role of spirituality, (3) our elevated rates of poverty, (4) our experience of sexual violence, and (5) the influence of colonialism. I identified the categories as points of significance slowly, over time, while immersed in the data of Risk & Resilience and the Two-Spirit Roundtable.

My familiarity with bisexuality's complexity helped form the foundation of our outreach strategy in Risk & Resilience, was featured in the recruitment video, and reflected in many of the survey questions. The complexity of bisexual identities helped me value the complexity of two-spirit identities and encouraged me to reflect this complexity in the design, recruitment, and data analysis during the Two-Spirit Roundtable. Perhaps because my doctoral training is in theology I had long noted bisexuality's engagement with spirituality. The spirituality of two-spirit identity was manifested in write-in responses from Aboriginal participants in Risk & Resilience and the way participants in the Two-Spirit Roundtable framed their lives and health as spiritually rooted, giving rise to the use of the Medicine Wheel for coding. The significance of poverty emerged quantitatively in participant data from Risk & Resilience, and qualitatively in data from both studies (Ross et al., 2016). The focus was also influenced by my experience of poverty as a child and young adult, and by my familiarity with research on bisexual incomes (Albelda, Badgett, Schneebaum, & Gates, 2009; C. S. Carpenter, 2005). Similarly, the significance of sexual violence for two-spirit people emerged quantitatively in Risk & Resilience, and a parallel was drawn for bisexuals more broadly from U.S. data (Walters, Chen, & Breiding, 2013).

The impact of colonization was apparent in the data from the Two-Spirit Roundtable, but an interest in measuring impacts of colonialism had been part of the survey development process with the Bisexual Community Advisory Committee in Risk & Resilience. The significance of colonialism for bisexuality was familiar to me from the writing of Elias Farajajé-Jones (2000; 1993). As I became more aware of the problems with subsuming two-spirit identity under the bisexual umbrella in Risk & Resilience I began to learn more about how our research framework and methods were reproducing settler colonialism, "the social processes and narratives that displace Native people while granting settlers belonging to native land and settler society" (Morgensen, 2010, p. 117). These five points of comparison are not exhaustive, and undoubtedly I could have explored more. For example, two-spirit and bisexual communities report high rates of substance use, undoubtedly interconnected with the issues I explore below.

Results: Five points of comparison

Complex identities

Bisexuality is a complex identity, encompassing people with a range of attractions and practices. Bisexual may describe participants who are attracted to men and women, those whose attractions include a range of genders, those for whom gender is not a primary factor in attraction, and those whose attractions change over time (Barker et al., 2012). Given all it encompasses, bisexuality has been likened to "pinning Jello to a wall" (Esterberg, 2002, p. 217). Lisa Diamond's 10-year longitudinal study (2008) found that women who identified as bisexual at the beginning of her study tended to switch between bisexual and unlabeled rather than having periods of lesbian or heterosexual identity. For some, bisexual identity may be the closest approximation to a sexuality that is unable to be named under the terms available. Such flexibility is useful. I did not need to relabel my sexuality when I became attracted to people who identified as genderqueer, androgynous, trans men, or trans women; my bisexuality accommodated these developments just fine.

The complexity of two-spirit identity makes it a challenge to define. Doe O'Brien Teengs (2008) has described two-spirit as "an Aboriginal person who is attracted to the same sex, or both sexes, and/or is transgendered or intersexual, and/or someone who possesses sacred gifts of the female/male spirit which exists in harmony in the one person" (p. 8). The range of people under the two-spirit umbrella makes it inappropriate to use the term as if it is synonymous with a single identity, such as bisexual, or trans. Still more is it not synonymous with queer, because two-spirit is not defined against traditional Indigenous gender or sexual roles (i.e., it is not "the Other").

Two-spirit identity is sometimes used to indicate gender difference, and sometimes to indicate sexual difference. In Risk & Resilience 42.8% of the Aboriginal participants reported two-spirit as both their sexual and gender identity. In the Two-Spirit Roundtable 39.4% of the participants reported two-spirit as their sexual identity, whereas 28.9% reported it as their gender. Two-spirit identity's inclusion of sexuality and gender may be appealing for Indigenous people. As a participant (two-spirit, gay; man, two-spirit) in the Two-Spirit Roundtable said, "I like the ambiguity that it has, so that you can say that you're two-spirit and it doesn't hold you as one thing. It still leaves people wondering, which I really like."

Two-spirit people are sometimes described as having a masculine and a feminine spirit. However, gender categories are not uniform across Indigenous; some recognize multiple genders (such as the Diné third gender, *nádleehí*), and two-spirit can be a way of recognizing those of us whose gender expression is distinctive. However, in many of our nations the idea of spirit having a gender, let alone two of them, is problematic. As a participant (two-spirit, gay; man, two-spirit) in the Two-Spirit Roundtable explained, "There are problems with the term itself, because I think it some way it implies that spirits have gender, and I don't think that spirits have gender. I think that's like – I don't think that it works that way." The elder (straight; man) who supported one of the talking circles in the Two-Spirit Roundtable also noted issues with the term:

> I have traditional spiritual problems with the notion of two-spirit because we are spirit.... So a spirit measured by number? Half spirits? Are there ¾ spirits.... On the other hand, all of us were born into a world and a dominant culture that insists on us being able to label ourselves. And if we are going to be labeling ourselves, let us at least be labeling ourselves with something of our own invention, however imperfect it may be.

Comments such as this highlight the contested nature of two-spirit identity (Greensmith & Giwa, 2013), and the way in which identities such as gay, lesbian, bisexual, or trans fail to reflect Indigenous gender complexity (Driskill, Finley, Gilley, & Morgensen, 2011).

Some participants in the Two-Spirit Roundtable reported issues related to how their gender was read by others. As one participant (unlabeled; *agokwe-nini*, two-spirit) said, "I struggle with it some days, especially accepting that male side... those stereotypes have been put there." Others seemed to integrate their ability to cross gender boundaries with relative ease. Another participant in the Two-Spirit Roundtable (*agokwe-nini*) said, "I am truly female and truly male. I dance men's traditional in pow-wow. I'm a fire-keeper. I'm also a kick-ass auntie and I'm a cook. All those things." Indigenous gender expression may draw harassment. A national survey of Canadian high school students found that over a third (39.1%) of the Aboriginal youth had been harassed due to their gender—a larger percentage than reported being harassed about their Aboriginality (28.4%) (Taylor et al., 2011). A number of scholars have noted the historical connection between colonial efforts to eradicate Indigenous gender diversity and efforts to eliminate and assimilate Indigenous nations (Arvin, Tuck, & Morrill, 2013; Driskill et al., 2011; Greensmith & Giwa, 2013; Morgensen, 2010; Smith, 2005, 2010).

To complicate matters further, some of us identify as two-spirit to signal our sexual, rather than gender difference. This understanding was endorsed quantitatively by participants in Risk & Resilience and the Two-Spirit Roundtable who identified their sexual identity as two-spirit, and also endorsed qualitatively by some of the people I interviewed in the Two-Spirit Roundtable who identified as two-spirit because they were attracted to members of the same sex. This use of 'two-spirit' may seem as if it operates as a synonym for lesbian, gay, or bisexual; however, Jenny L. Davis (2014) warned against assuming that the meaning Indigenous people attach to such labels is the same as those used by the dominant culture. J. L. Davis (2014) suggests that Indigenous people may view gender and sexuality as "potentially overlapping states" rather than as binary categories (p. 62).

When asked, "What things do you like about being bisexual?" one Aboriginal participant (two-spirit, queer, homoflexible; two-spirit, genderqueer) in Risk & Resilience wrote, "It befits my trickster hybrid experience in the world & complicates our understandings of intersecting identities." Another, (two-spirit, bisexual, pansexual, queer; two-spirit, genderqueer, transman) reported, "I feel connected to my two-spirit ancestors." These statements show how two-spirit people are integrating their cultural identities with their sexual or gender identities in ways that defy simple definitions.

Perhaps unsurprisingly, two-spirit participants found it difficult to communicate the complexity of their identity to others, making it difficult to feel recognized. A Two-Spirit Roundtable participant who identifies as *agokwe-nini* said, "Some people get confused … because they think it means I'm trans, and it's not how I identify." A Risk & Resilience participant (two-spirit, bisensual, bisexual, fluid, omnisexual, pansexual, queer, questioning; two-spirit, genderqueer, androgynous) wrote, "identifying as 2-spirit is sometimes frustrating … so many non-Native people tend to parse 2-spirit to mean gay and completely ignore the gender implications." Another (two-spirit, bisexual, fluid, pansexual, queer; two-spirit, bigendered, crossdresser, genderqueer, trans man) remarked, "I feel as if I seem rather complicated to others, but not to myself. 'Normal' people get to seem simple."

Despite their shared complexity, bisexual and two-spirit identity are not interchangeable. Some participants in Risk & Resilience highlighted the distinctiveness of two-spirit identity from bisexuality. One (two-spirit, bisexual, pansexual, queer; two-spirit, genderqueer, trans man) remarked, "The term bisexual does not do justice to the ways I understand my gender, sex, sexuality, and the roles and responsibilities related to being two-spirit." Another (two-spirit, bisexual, pansexual, queer; two-spirit, genderqueer, transman) wrote, "I am often invisibilized by false categories created by settler-colonial Canada making me into something I am not," highlighting the issue of how we categorize individuals and their data.

As researchers we may be tempted to reduce two-spirit identity to make it fit into predetermined colonial categories for data analysis. As a result, we rarely have data on two-spirit people and our health. Yet excluding us from analysis because our numbers are small feeds two-spirit identity erasure as well as the erasure of Indigenous nations and lives (Arvin et al., 2013; Driskill et al., 2011; Greensmith & Giwa, 2013; Morgensen, 2010; Smith, 2005, 2010). Such issues are familiar to those who conduct bisexual research. J. L. Davis (2014) could just as easily be speaking about bisexuality when she describes two-spirit identity as "complex, multilayered, and, at times contradictory" (p. 62). If we ask research participants to name their identities we have a responsibility to work honestly with the complexity of those identities, even if they resist simple analyses.

Spirituality

Two-spirit identity carries a spiritual meaning, and spirituality may be an important determinant of health for Indigenous sexual and gender minority people more broadly. In a study of the health of trans people in Ontario, 44% of the Aboriginal participants reported having an Aboriginal spirituality and 56% indicated that they were fairly, quite, or extremely religious (Scheim et al., 2013). Spirituality, especially in an Indigenous framework, is not easily equivalent to religiosity. Spirituality is about our place in a web of relationships with other people, with the animals that share our territories, and with the land itself. As two-spirit scholar Alex Wilson (2008) explains, Indigenous "language and culture are rooted in this fundamental truth: that every living creature and everything that acts in and on this world is spiritually meaningful" (p. 193).

In precontact Indigenous cultures a third or fourth gender identity was reported to emerge in response to events in the spirit world, accessed through dreams or visions. Michael Tlanusta Garrett and Bob Barret (2003) emphasize that two-spirit is a spiritual role rather than an identity:

> In many Native traditions, the Two Spirit was looked on as having the ability to walk in two worlds, physical and spiritual, thereby having the ability to move between worlds to learn and teach about balance. As such, Two Spirit people were highly revered as medicine persons, leaders, and intermediaries. They were an integral part of tribal society just like anyone else and not looked down as being abnormal in any way. They were seen as an asset to tribal life, not a liability that would erode the community's stability. (p. 134)

Our integration into our Indigenous communities is one of the features that distinguishes two-spirit people from identities like bisexual or trans. Two-spirit identity incorporates "culture … spirituality, community and relationship to the land" (Wilson, 2008, p. 193). Given this, even the practice of categorizing two-spirit people together may be challenged since each of us brings meanings to the identity that are rooted in our own Indigenous nation. Is a participant who identifies as *agokwe*, for example, similar enough to someone who identifies as *nádleehí* to be grouped together for analysis? Or are we erasing important differences?

While numerous religious organizations welcome LGBTQ people, spirituality has been peripheral to gay, lesbian, trans, and queer identity. Christian De La Huerta has even described queerness as "the only liberation movement that is not spiritually inspired" (K. Davis, 2006). To a certain degree, bisexuality has broken this pattern of secularity. Spirituality features prominently in bisexual anthologies, in some cases making up to a quarter of each book (Atkins, 2002; Bisexual Anthology Collective, 1995; Hutchins & Ka'ahumanu, 1991; Ochs, 2005; Suresha & Chvany, 2006; Tucker, Highleyman & Kaplan, 1995). Those essays approach spirituality as a solution to binary constructions of gender, sex, and sexuality that form the roots of biphobia. Section titles such as "Bridge Building in Bisexual Spirit" or "Healing the Splits" reflect this approach (Hutchins & Ka'ahumanu, 1991; Suresha & Chavny, 2006). In their introduction to a special edition of the *Journal of*

Bisexuality on spirituality, Loraine Hutchins and Sharif Williams (2010) note that "one theme for bisexual people in their spiritual lives is being able to heal the painful splits ... between public and private, female and male, gay and straight, closeted and being out, body and soul, sacred and profane" (p. 7). The spirituality represented in bisexual anthologies "is the force that draws people together and makes loving across socially constructed and politically policed boundaries possible" (Robinson, 2014c, p. 651).

To the degree that bisexuality is framed as a sexual expression of a spiritual reality, it is similar to two-spirit identity. Yet while bisexuality is an occasionally spiritual identity, two-spirit identity is a predominantly spiritual identity. The difference is of degree, but also of kind. Bisexual anthologies include essays from Jewish, Christian, and Buddhist perspectives but are primarily weighted toward neo-paganism. Two-spirit identity has its roots in Indigenous spiritual traditions that are constantly appropriated by settlers, including those under the LGBTQ umbrella. While entering data on a pilot study of bisexual mental health, for example, I noted that more people reported a two-spirited identity than reported being Aboriginal. As a two-spirit person I agree with Loraine Hutchins and Lani Ka'ahumanu (1991) when they write, "We call the old tribal polymorphous ways back into being and assert that they are necessary" (p. 92), even as I rush to assert that our "tribal" ways are for ourselves alone.

Poverty

There is a dearth of data on the prevalence or impact of poverty among two-spirit and bisexual people. However, preliminary evidence suggests that bisexual and two-spirit people have elevated rates of poverty. The few studies that have examined bisexual people separately suggest that bisexuals have lower incomes (C. S. Carpenter, 2005) and are more likely to live in poverty (Albelda et al., 2009) than our gay and lesbian peers. A recent study of bisexual people age 25 and older found that 25.7% were living below the low income cut-off (the point at which a family devotes a larger than average share of its income to food, shelter, and clothing) (Ross et al., 2016). This issue is intersectional as well, with bisexual people who are Indigenous facing an even greater poverty risk. In Risk & Resilience bisexual people below the low income cutoff were more likely to identify as Aboriginal ($p = .05$) compared to bisexuals living above the cutoff (Ross et al., 2016). Also in that study, 65% of the Aboriginal participants reported making less than $20,000 CDN (approx. $15,300 USD) annually, and many reported relying on social services or public aid as their primary source of income (Ross et al., 2016). In the Trans PULSE study 47% of the Aboriginal participants were living below the low income cutoff (Scheim et al., 2013).

Poverty has a direct negative impact on our health. Lori Ross and colleagues (2016) found that bisexuals living below the low income cutoff had significantly higher scores for depression and post-traumatic stress disorder symptoms than their peers. Although the numbers of Aboriginal participants in Risk & Resilience was too low to produce statistical associations between income and mental health, the majority (63%) reported having an unmet mental health need within the past year. Of those with an unmet need, 37% reported not being able to afford treatment. Poverty also has an indirect health impact, by shaping our ability to participate in LGBTQ community and benefit from the support those social connections provide. As one participant (male, gay, two-spirit) in the Two-Spirit Roundtable remarked, "I noticed when you quit drinking your friends disappear. <Laughs>. You ever notice that? You don't have money or you quit lending money or you quit drinking and all your friends are gone." As Fiona Meyer-Cook and Diane Labelle (2003) note, a lack of resources for two-spirit people may cause or exacerbate poverty:

> With few Two-Spirit people knowing where and how to gain access to 'Two-Spirit friendly' Elders, role models, healthy lifestyle alternatives and inclusive cultural spaces, many 'fall through the cracks' and end up on city streets, living in poverty with poorer health and with greater risk of becoming lost and in pain. (p. 40)

Bisexual and two-spirit people may experience similar marginalization (albeit to different degrees), within sexual and gender minority communities, and within society more broadly.

Poverty is a result of economic exploitation, a significant element of colonial domination (Hamilton, 2010). Professor of American Indian Studies Dian Million has noted the extent to which colonial processes of control, such as Canada's Indian Act, intentionally create and exacerbate Indigenous poverty for women and their children by thwarting access to their treaty rights (Million, 2013). Classifying two-spirit people as bisexual without controlling for factors unique to two-spirit people may skew poverty statistics by including people whose income is affected by colonialism and racism as well as heterosexism or biphobia. As well, poverty is a factor shaping our vulnerability to sexual violence (Million, 2013), and has, along with lack of public transportation, been identified as a key factor in the disappearance and murder of Indigenous women along The Highway of Tears (Canadian Press, 2014).

Sexual violence

Two-spirit and bisexual people share a high exposure to sexual violence rooted in colonial heterosexist and cissexist norms (Greensmith & Giwa, 2013; Morgensen, 2010; Smith, 2005). A national study conducted in the United States found that 46.1% of bisexual women had been raped compared with 17.4% of heterosexual women and 13.1% of lesbians (Walters et al., 2013). bisexual men and women also reported the highest rates of intimate partner violence (Walters et al., 2013).

Several theorists have noted that bisexual women in particular, are presented in television and social media as if their bisexuality signals sexual availability and interest. Wan-Hsiu Sunny Tsai (2010) notes that when they appear at all, bisexual women are depicted in commercial media as hedonistic, promiscuous, and sexually available. Similarly, bisexual activist Shiri Eisner (2013, 2014) argues that bisexual women who are bisexual are framed as hypsersexual objects for the male gaze. What is represented, Eisner argues, is a phallocentric fantasy of female sexual availability projected onto bisexual women, a fantasy she associates with biohobic violence (p. 162).

Although the research is sparse, studies have also found high rates of sexual violence among Indigenous people who are two-spirit or LGB. In a study of gay, bisexual, and two-spirit men in New York City, 10% had been sexually assaulted by a partner and 45% had been sexually assaulted by someone other than a partner (Simoni, Walters, Balsam, & Meyers, 2006). Similarly, a study of lesbian, bisexual, and two-spirit American Indian and Alaskan Native women found that 85% had been sexually assaulted, which was associated with worse overall mental and physical health (Lehavot, Walters & Simoni, 2009). This pattern has also been found in Canadian data. In Risk & Resilience, for example, 58% of the Aboriginal participants reported experiencing the use of sexual force before age 16. The Trans PULSE study found that 43% of the Aboriginal participants in their study had experienced physical or sexual violence (Scheim et al., 2013).

Many factors combine to increase our risk of being targeted for sexual assault, including our poverty, racialization, and gender. Undoubtedly, a key risk factor is also colonialism "Rape and sexual violence," explains Million (2013), "have always been normative to the subjugation of colonized peoples" (p. 38). This is certainly shown in the available data; two national surveys in Canada found that Aboriginal women had four times the odds of experiencing violence compared with non-Aboriginal women, even after controlling for age, education, marital status, alcohol use, unemployment, and patriarchal dominance (Brownridge, 2008).

Sexual violence is intimately linked with the violence done to Indigenous gender systems by Christian colonialism's imposition of a hierarchical gender binary (Arvin et al., 2013; Driskill et al., 2011; Greensmith & Giwa, 2013; Morgensen, 2010; Smith, 2005, 2010). Sexual violence was endemic to the residential and boarding school systems into which Indigenous children were forced as part of a broad assimilation project in Canada and the United States. A study by Evans-Campbell, Walters, Pearson, and Campbell (2012) found that 29.3% of their two-spirit participants who had attended boarding school reported being sexually harmed there. Sexual violation may be an experience shared by multiple generations within Indigenous families, and by multiple members within a generation. As a participant in The Two-Spirit Roundtable (man; gay, two-spirit) said when speaking about his own experience of sexual violence, "When I was abused, who was in that room with me? My sister was there with me. We were both sexually abused. It wasn't just me; it was her too."

Data analyses related to sexual violence faces the same issues as analyses related to poverty; if two-spirit participants are at greater risk of being targeted by sexual offenders than including them under the bisexual umbrella in data analysis may inflate the statistics on sexual assault experienced by people under the bisexual umbrella, as well as denying the role played by colonialism and racialized sexism in shaping sexual violence.

Colonization

Two-spirit identity is one way of reclaiming Indigenous cultural elements that have been damaged by colonialism (Driskill et al., 2011). The transmission of principles, Indigenous values, practices, and identities from one generation to the next has been termed cultural continuity. In First Nations communities cultural continuity has been found to reduce negative health outcomes such as suicide (Chandler & Lalonde, 1998) and diabetes (Oster, Grier, Lightning, Mayan, & Toth, 2014). Two-spirit identity can connect us with our culture in ways that serve our health (Robinson, 2014a, 2014b, 2015). Two-spirit identity locates us firmly within our Indigenous nations and signals that the meaning of our gender or sexuality is to be found there, not in colonial systems with claims to universality (Robinson, 2012). Alex Wilson (2008) noted that though LGBT identity has been about individual difference from the mainstream norm, two-spirit identity had been about cultural belonging. Coming out as LGBT, she explains, "is typically a declaration of an independent identity," whereas two-spirit identity "reflects Aboriginal peoples' process of 'coming in' to an empowered identity that integrates their sexuality, culture, gender and all other aspects of who they understand and know themselves to be" (p. 197). Scholars have already questioned the facile inclusion of two-spirit people within LGBTQ communities (Arvin et al., 2013; Morgensen, 2010) and homonationalist discourses (Greensmith & Giwa, 2013). Even within CBR projects that aspire to be decolonizing, inclusion itself may be a process that is "central to hierarchal power" (Arvin et al., 2013, p. 14).

Although I generally consider colonization an element that distinguishes two-spirit from bisexual identity, some scholars have disagreed. Kenneth Hamilton (2010) argues that "colonization has always historically meant the targeting of queer sexualities and spiritualties, the crushing of fluid sexual behavior to establish a heteronorm" (p. 122), and a number of scholars have identified heteropatriarchy as central to settler colonialism (Arvin et al., 2013; Driskill et al., 2011; Greensmith & Giwa, 2013; Morgensen, 2010; Smith, 2005, 2010). Bisexual theologian Ibrahim Abdurrahman Farajajé (née Elias Farajajé-Jones) argued that bisexual bodies and minds are colonized by heteropatriarchy, which focuses our energy on assimilating into the heterosexual mainstream. He described bisexuals as "victims of forced relocations from the very core of our being," and asserted that only decolonizing ourselves psychologically would enable each of us to express our full complexity (Farajajé-Jones, 2000, p. 16). Yet we need to be aware that the interlocking systems of oppression do not impact everyone to the same degree or in the same ways.

As researchers we must rise to the challenge of incorporating intersectionality into our data analyses (Robinson, 2015; Robinson & Ross, 2013). As J. Andrew Baker (2014) explains:

> it's important when you're looking at Aboriginal LGBT identified or two-spirited individuals, that they have two major sources of trauma. They have the multigenerational impacts of residential school and colonization and what's happened to them as an aboriginal person. And then they have a multigenerational four or five hundred year history of what's happened in queer community in colonial nations.

Both of these sources of trauma have colonial roots. As a participant (two-spirit, bisexual, pansexual, queer; two-spirit, genderqueer, transman) in Risk & Resilience wrote. "All of the ways in which I am oppressed stem from the same source of violence: colonization." Hamilton (2010) made important connections between the Christian colonialism in North America and that in Africa and raised important issues about gay (inter)nationalism. Yet these instances are similar not because the victims are similar, but because the oppressors and their ideologies are. Too often such comparisons treat the 40 "sodomites" murdered by Vasco Núñez de Balboa and his men as if they are easily identified as queers, and as if their Indigeneity and racialization were incidental. I am wary of any sleight of hand that replaces Indigenous peoples with queers, as if it is queer people that have borne the brunt of colonialism.

Conclusion: Rain and the staying power of umbrellas

At the beginning of this article I asked what similarities existed between bisexuality and two-spirit identity and pondered whether they were strong enough to justify bringing two-spirit participants under the bisexual umbrella. I see a number of parallels in how bisexual and two-spirit identities are marginalized and oppressed, and Indigenous and ally scholars have identified colonialism as a root cause of many of the systemic oppressions at work. Yet ignoring the key differences between these two identities risks impacting data analysis in ways that obscure peoples' lived experiences of those oppressions. More importantly, it risks affecting the people themselves in ways that reinscribe and magnify their oppression.

Two-spirit people are present in bisexual community, and we experience biphobia, heterosexism, and monosexism, due to the ways our two-spirit and other identities challenge colonial categories. Like bisexuals, we also experience erasure, although unlike bisexuals it is our cultural identity as well as our gender and/or sexual identity that is being erased. Those of us who identify as bisexual and as two-spirit may experience multiple erasures on a daily basis. As a participant (female, two-spirit) in Risk & Resilience reported, "I feel that my identity as a white-looking Aboriginal femme bisexual renders me invisible much of the time." Although the research I conducted occurred within a Canadian context, the border distinguishing Canada and the United States is not an Indigenous one, and in fact cuts directly through some of our nations. Moreover, both colonial powers have been complicit in supporting one another's Imperial projects, and have enacted similar laws, evoked similar claims to Manifest Destiny, and resorted to similar tactics to justify ongoing repression of Indigenous sovereignty.

As researchers we must reflect carefully about which type of data we collect from Indigenous people, how we group it, and what to do with small numbers and associated low statistical power. Each of these decisions is an ethical choice. The category 'Aboriginal,' for example, is an term defined by the colonial Government of Canada to include three very distinct types of peoples (First Nations, Inuit, and Métis), and does not reflect Indigenous self-understanding, The term 'First Nations' is itself an artificial construct, grouping together distinct nations as if we are essentially the same. Apart from the issue of how to categorize us, the choice of how to analyze those categories is also an ethical one. If, for example, researchers categorize us as a racialized population they ignore the role of colonialism in favor of racism, despite our nations including many who, like me, move through the world with the privileges incurred by having White skin. If we are categorized as a nonracialized group then we erase the very real impact of racism in the lives of many Indigenous people. Likewise, to fold two-spirit under various LGBTQ umbrellas assumes that indigenous identity is essentially the same as identities rooted in the colonial sex and gender matrix. Although there is evidence that bisexual and two-spirit people suffer from these binaries in similar ways, these identities come from very different social systems and communicate different things.

Health researchers like myself must determine whether we will classify two-spirit people by our sex assigned at birth, the masculinity or femininity of our gender identity, how we perceive our own gender, or how our gender is interpreted by others, and we should have clear rationales for how this decision relates to Indigenous peoples' determinants of health. It is past time we began asking how our participants' gender is perceived by others in surveys that examine the impact of gender on health, especially because this perception is shaped so thoroughly by settler colonialism.

The work of distinguishing bisexual from two-spirit identities, despite their similarities, has implications for two-spirit activists attempting to counter discourses of assimilation and erasure, as well as for bisexual allies wishing to avoid replaying settler colonial scripts. More research is needed into how discourses of normativity—including binormativity— and those of nationalism—including bisexual community rhetoric—reflect and expand discourses of settler nationalism. As bisexual identity received increasing attention in news and social media, bisexual communities, and those of us whose research is accountable to them, must grapple with the ways in which we have and continue to participate in the logics of settler colonialism. We must, for example, grapple with our own history of endorsing Whiteness as a central value (Farajajé-Jones, 1993; Perez, 1995; Rust, 1995), and question how binormativity and bisexual identity politics are predicated on Imperial approaches to Indigenous people and the land.

Health services, if they are to be responsive to the needs of bisexual and two-spirit clients, need to be aware of the issues affecting our well-being (such as poverty, and sexual violence), as well as factors that may shape our resilience (such as spirituality). Services must also be consciously aware of the colonial root of oppressions such as monosexism and biphobia without assuming that colonialism and its related oppressions affect all groups to the same degree or in the same ways. To use the umbrella metaphor, colonization may be the rain that beats upon both bisexual and two-spirit people, but the deluge hits us to different degrees and we may find that we are under different umbrellas for very good reasons. Two-spirit identity is an umbrella that Indigenous people have made ourselves, designed for the kind of downpour we have been experiencing since colonialism began.

Acknowledgments

The author wishes to acknowledge the participants in the Two-Spirit Roundtable, and those whose wisdom and hard work made the study possible, particularly two-spirit elder, Blu Waters, two-spirit community members Louis Esme Cruz, and Sharp Dopler. Thanks also to the Evidence Exchange Network, the Ontario Aboriginal HIV/AIDS Strategy, and the Ontario federation of Indigenous Friendship Centres. I also wish to acknowledge the investigators, coinvestigators, and advisors of the Risk & Resilience Study, including Lori Ross, Greta Bauer, Cheryl Dobinson, Jenna MacKay, Ishwar Persad, and Loralee Gillis. The author also wishes to thank Shamara Baidoobonso and Melissa A. MacLeod for their work data cleaning and coding, the members of the Risk & Resilience Bisexual Community Advisory Committee (particularly Blu Waters and Louis Esme Cruz), and all of the staff and students of the Re:searching for LGBTQ Health team who contributed to these projects (see www.lgbtqhealth.ca).

References

Albelda, R., Badgett, M. V., Schneebaum, A., & Gates, G. (2009). *Poverty in the lesbian, gay, and bisexual community.* Los Angeles, CA: Williams Institute.

Arvin, M., Tuck, E., & Morrill, A. (2013). Decolonizing feminism: Challenging connections between settler colonialism and heteropatriarchy. *Feminist Formations, 25*(1), 8–34. doi:10.1353/ff.2013.0006

Atkins, D. (2002). *Bisexual women in the twenty-first centur.* New York, NY: Haworth Press.

Baker, J. A. (interviewee) (2014, February 18). *J. Andrew Baker* [Audio podcast]. Retrieved from http://lgbtqhealth.ca/projects/two-spiritedpodcasts.php?ap=1#JAndrewBaker

Barker, M., Richards, C., Jones, R., Bowes-Catton, H., & Plowman, T. (2012). *The bisexuality report: Bisexual inclusion in LGBT equality and diversity.* Milton Keynes, England: Open University, Centre for Citizenship, Identity and Governance.

Bauer, G. R., Flanders, C., MacLeod, M. A., & Ross, L. E. (2016). Occurrence of multiple mental health or substance use outcomes among bisexuals: A respondent-driven sampling study. *BMC Public Health, 16*(1), 497–508. doi:10.1186/s12889-016-3173-z

Bisexual Anthology Collective. (1995). *Plural desires: Writing bisexual women's realities.* Toronto, Canada: Sister Vision Press.

Blackwood, E. (1997). Native American genders and sexualities: Beyond anthropological models and misrepresentations. In S. E. Jacobs, W. Thomas, & S. Lang (Eds.), *Two-spirited people: Native American gender identity, sexuality, and spirituality* (pp. 284–294). Urbana, IL: University of Illinois Press.

Brownridge, D. A. (2008). Understanding the elevated risk of partner violence against Aboriginal women: A comparison of two nationally representative surveys of Canada. *Journal of Family Violence, 23*(5), 353–367. doi:10.1007/s10896-008-9160-0

Bullough, V. L. (1976). *Sexual variance in society and history.* Chicago, IL: University of Chicago Press.

Canadian Press. (2014). B.C. Highway of Tears study polls hitchhikers' habits. Retrieved from http://www.cbc.ca/news/canada/british-columbia/b-c-highway-of-tears-study-polls-hitchhikers-habits-1.2653808

Carpenter, C. S. (2005). Self-reported sexual orientation and earnings: Evidence from California. *Industrial & Labor Relations Review, 58*(2), 258–273. doi:10.1177/001979390505800205

Carpenter, R. M. (2011). Womanish men and manlike women: The Native American two-spirit as warrior. In S. Slater & F. A. Yarbough (Eds.), *Gender and sexuality in Indigenous North America 1400–1850* (pp. 146–164). Columbus, SC: University of South Carolina.

Castleden, H., Garvin, T., Huu-ay-aht First Nation. (2008). Modifying photovoice for community-based participatory Indigenous research. *Social Science & Medicine, 66*(6), 1393–1405. http://dx.doi.org/10.1016/j.socscimed.2007.11.030

Castleden, H., Morgan, V. S., & Lamb, C. (2012). "I spent the first year drinking tea": Exploring Canadian university researchers' perspectives on community-based participatory research involving Indigenous peoples. *Canadian Geographer, 56*(2), 160–179. DOI:10.1111/j.1541-0064.2012.00432.x

CBC News, The Early Edition. (2015, January 9). Harlan Pruden finds healing for LGBT First Nations in tradition. *CBC News, The Early Edition.* Retrieved from http://www.cbc.ca/news/canada/british-columbia/harlan-pruden-finds-healing-for-lgbt-first-nations-in-tradition-1.2894254

Centre for Addiction and Mental Health. (2012, July 19). *Risk & Resilience Study of Bisexual Mental Health* [Video file]. Retrieved from https://www.youtube.com/watch?v=AEJFKjDlOeo

Chandler, M. J., & Lalonde, C. (1998). Cultural continuity as a hedge against suicide in Canada's First Nations. *Transcultural Psychiatry, 35*, 191–219. doi:10.1177/136346159803500202

Constitution Act. (1982). being Schedule B to the Canada Act 1982 (UK), 1982, c 35(2) a.

Cromwell, J. (1997). Traditions of gender diversity and sexualities: A female-to-male transgendered perspective. In S. E. Jacobs, W. Thomas, & S. Lang (Eds.), *Two-spirited people: Native American gender identity, sexuality, and spirituality* (pp. 119–142). Urbana, IL: University of Illinois Press.

Davis, J. L. (2014). More than just 'gay indians'. In L. Zimman, J. Davis, and J. RaclawJ (Eds.). *Queer excursions: Retheorizing binaries in language, gender, and sexuality* (pp. 62–80). New York, NY: Oxford University Press.

Davis, K. (2006, October 5). Secular LGBT groups should embrace spiritual gays, leader says". *Bay Area Reporter.* Retrieved from http://www.ebar.com/news/article.php?sec=news&article=1219

Diamond, L. M. (2008). Female bisexuality from adolescence to adulthood: results from a 10-year longitudinal study. *Developmental Psychology, 44*(1), 5–14. doi:10.1037/0012-1649.44.1.5

Driskill, Q. L., Finley, C., Gilley, B. J., & Morgensen, S. L. (2011). Introduction. In Q. L. Driskill, C. Finley, B. J. Gilley, & S. L. Morgensen. (Eds.), *Queer Indigenous studies: Critical interventions in theory, politics, and literature* (pp. 1–28). Tuscon, AZ: University of Arizona Press.

Eisner, S. (2011). *The bisexual umbrella*. Retrieved from https://radicalbi.wordpress.com/2011/11/23/the-bisexual-umbrella/

Eisner, S. (2013). *Bi: Notes for a bisexual revolution*. Berkeley, CA: Seal Press.

Eisner, S. (2014, May 7). Orphan Black's Delphine and the dangers of the bisexual femme fatale. *Autostraddle*. http://www.autostraddle.com/orphan-blacks-delphine-and-the-dangers-of-the-bisexual-femme-fatale-236775/

Esterberg, K. G. (2002). The bisexual menace: Or, will the real bisexual please stand up? In D. Richardson & S. Seidman (Eds.), *Handbook of lesbian and gay studies* (pp. 215–228). Thousand Oaks, CA: Sage.

Evans-Campbell, T., Walters, K. L., Pearson, C. R., & Campbell, C. D. (2012). Indian boarding school experience, substance use, and mental health among urban two-spirit American Indian/Alaska Natives. *American Journal of Drug and Alcohol Abuse, 38*(5), 421–427. doi:10.3109/00952990.2012.701358

Farajaje-Jones, E. (1993). Breaking silence: Toward an in-the-life theology. In J.H. Cone & G.S. Wilmore (Eds.), Black theology: A documentary history [Volume two: 1980–1992] (pp. 139–159). Maryknoll, NY: Orbis.

Farajajé-Jones, E. (2000). 'Loving queer' We're all a big mix of possibilities of desire just waiting to happen. *The Family: A Magazine for Lesbians, Gays, Bisexuals, and their Relations*, *6*(1), 14–21.

Flanders, C. E., LeBreton, M. E., Robinson, M., Bian, J., & Caravaca-Morea, J. A. (In Press). Defining bisexuality: Young bisexual and pansexual people[1]s voices. *Journal of Bisexuality*. doi:http://dx.doi.org/10.1080/15299716.2016.1227016

Galupo, M. P., Ramirez, J. L., & Pulice-Farrow, L. (In press). "Regardless of their gender": Descriptions of sexual identity among bisexual, pansexual, and queer identified individuals. *Journal of Bisexuality*. doi:http://dx.doi.org/10.1080/15299716.2016.1228491

Galupo, M. P., Mitchell, R. C., & Davis, K. S. (2015). Sexual minority self-identification: Multiple identities and complexity. *Psychology of Sexual Orientation and Gender Diversity, 2*(4), 355–364. http://dx.doi.org/10.1037/sgd0000131

Garber, M. B. (1995). *Vice Versa: Bisexuality and the eroticism of everyday life*. New York, NY: Simon & Schuster.

Garrett, M. T., & Barret, B. (2003). Two spirit: Counseling Native American gay, lesbian, and bisexual people. *Journal of Multicultural Counseling and Development, 31*(2), 131–142. http://dx.doi.org/10.1080/15299711003609799

Greenberg, D. F. (1990). *The construction of homosexuality*. University of Chicago Press.

Greensmith, C., & Giwa, S. (2013). Challenging settler colonialism in contemporary queer politics: Settler homonationalism, Pride Toronto, and two-spirit subjectivities. *American Indian Culture and Research Journal, 37*(2), 129–148. doi:http://dx.doi.org/10.17953/aicr.37.2.p4q2r84l12735117

Gunn Allen, P. (1989). Lesbians in American Indian cultures. In M. B. Duberman, V. Vicinus, & G. Chauncey, Jr.. (Eds.), *Hidden from history: Reclaiming the gay and lesbian past* (pp. 106–118). New York, NY: New American Library.

Hamilton, K. (2010). Colonial legacies, decolonized spirits: Balboa, Ugandan martyrs and AIDS solidarity today. *Journal of Bisexuality, 10*(1/2), 121–136. doi:10.1080/15299711003609799

Hatcher, A., Bartlett, C., Marshall, A., & Marshall, M. (2009). Two-eyed seeing in the classroom environment: Concepts, approaches, and challenges. *Canadian Journal of Science, Mathematics and Technological Education, 9*, 141–153. doi:10.1080/14926150903118342

Hutchins, L., & Ka'ahumanu, L. (1991). *Bi any other name: Bisexual people speak out*. Boston, MA: Alyson Publications.

Hutchins, L. & Williams, H. S. (2010). Our hearts still hold these intimate connections: An introduction to the spiritualities special issue of the *Journal of Bisexuality*. *Journal of Bisexuality, 10*(1/2), 4–17. http://dx.doi.org/10.1080/15299711003609583

Institute for Integrative Science & Health. (2012). *Two-eyed seeing*. Retrieved from http://www.integrative science.ca/Principles/TwoEyedSeeing/

Israel, B., Eng, E., Schultz, A., & Parker, E. (2005). *Methods in community-based participatory action research for health*. San Francisco: CA: John Wiley and Sons.

Kovach, M. (2010). Conversation method in Indigenous research. *First People Child & Family Review, 5*(1), 40–48. Retrieved from https://fncaringsociety.com/sites/default/files/online-journal/vol5num1/Kovach_pp40.pdf

Lang, S. (1998). *Men as women, women as men: Changing gender in Native American cultures*. Austin, TX: University of Texas Press.

Lehavot, K., Walters, K. L., & Simoni, J. M. (2009). Abuse, mastery, and health among lesbian, bisexual, and two-spirit American Indian and Alaska Native women. *Cultural Diversity and Ethnic Minority Psychology, 15*(3), 275–284.

LeVay, S. (2010). *Gay, straight, and the reason why: The science of sexual orientation*. New York, NY: Oxford University Press.

MacLeod, M., Bauer, G., Ross, L., Robinson, M., & MacKay, J. (2015). Biphobia and anxiety among bisexuals in Ontario, Canada. *Journal of Gay & Lesbian Mental Health, 19*, 217–243. doi:10.1080/19359705.2014.1003121

McGregor, D. (2008). Linking traditional ecological knowledge and Western science: Aboriginal perspectives from the 2000 State of The Lakes Ecosystem Conference. *Canadian Journal of Native Studies, 28*(1), 139–158. Retrieved from https://www.nwclimatescience.org/sites/default/files/2013bootcamp/readings/McGregor_2008.pdf

Meyer-Cook, F., & Labelle, D. (2003). Namaji: Two-spirit organizing in Montreal, Canada. *Journal of Gay and Lesbian Social Services, 16*(1), 26–51. http://dx.doi.org/10.1300/J041v16n01_02

Million, D. (2013). *Therapeutic nations: Healing in an age of indigenous human rights*. Tucson, AZ: University of Arizona Press.

Mitchell, R. C., Davis, K. S., & Galupo, M. P. (2015). Comparing perceived experiences of prejudice among self-identified plurisexual individuals. *Psychology and Sexuality, 6*, 245–257. http://dx.doi.org/10.1080/19419899.2014.940372

Morgensen, S. L. (2010). Settler homonationalism: Theorizing settler colonialism within queer modernities. *GLQ: A Journal of Lesbian and Gay Studies, 16*(1/2), 105–131. doi:10.1215/10642684-2009-015

O'Brien-Teengs, D. (2008). Two spirit women (2nd Edition). 2-Spirited People of the 1st Nations. Retrieved from http://www.2spirits.com/PDFolder/Two%20Spirit%20Women.pdf

Ochs, R. (2005). *Getting bi: Voices of bisexuals around the world*. Boston, MA: Bisexual Resource Center.

Oster, R. T., Grier, A., Lightning, R., Mayan, M. J., & Toth, E. L. (2014). Cultural continuity, traditional Indigenous language, and diabetes in Alberta First Nations: A mixed methods study. *International Journal for Equity in Health, 13*(1), 92–103. doi:10.1186/s12939-014-0092-4

Perez, L. M. (1995). Go ahead: Make my movement. In N. Tucker, L. Highleyman and R. Kaplan, (Eds.), *Bisexual Politics: Theories, queries and visions* (pp. 109–114). New York, NY: Harrington Press.

Robertson, D. V. (1997). I ask you to listen to who I am. In S.E. Jacobs, W. Thomas, & S. Lang (Ed.), *Two-spirited people: Native American gender identity, sexuality, and spirituality*. (pp. 228–235). Urbana, IL: University of Illinois Press.

Robinson, M. (2012, June 6). Two-spirited sexuality and white universality. *Postcolonial Networks*. Retrieved from http://postcolonialnetworks.com/2012/06/02/two-spirited/

Robinson, M. (2014a). A hope to lift both my spirits: Preventing bisexual erasure in First Nations schools. *Journal of Bisexuality, 14*(1), 18–35. doi:https://doi.org/10.1080/15299716.2014.872457

Robinson, M. (2014b). Two-spirited sexuality and resisting assimilation. In D. Gosse (Ed.), *Out proud: Stories of pride, courage and social justice* (pp. 144–149). St. John's, Canada: Breakwater Books.

Robinson, M. (2014c). Bisexual people. In A. Thatcher (Ed.), *The Oxford handbook of theology, sexuality and gender* (pp. 640–656). London, UK: Oxford Press.

Robinson, M. (2015). Standing in the intersection: Aboriginality, sexuality and mental health. In H. Klonaris & A. Rabiyah (Eds.), *Writing the walls down: A convergence of LGBTQ voices* (pp. 31–41). Oakland CA: Trans-Genre Press.

Robinson, M., Plante, I., MacLeod, M. A., Cruz, L., & Banji, N., on behalf of Re:searching for LGBTQ Health. (2016). Experiences of Aboriginal People in the Risk and Resilience Study [Fact sheet]. Toronto, Canada: Centre for Addiction and Mental Health. Retrieved from http://lgbtqhealth.ca/projects/docs/riskresiliencebisexual-factsheet-aboriginal-community.pdf .

Robinson, M., & Ross, L. E. (2013). Gender and sexual minorities: Intersecting inequalities and health. *Ethnicity and Inequalities in Health and Social Care, 6*(4), 91–96. doi:10.1108/EIHSC-01-2014-0003

Robinson, M., Sanches, M., & MacLeod, M. (2016). Prevalence and mental health correlates of cannabis use among a networked sample of bisexual women in Ontario, Canada. *Journal of Bisexuality, 16*(2), 181–202. doi:10.1080/15299716.2016.1147402

Ross, L. E., Bauer, G. R., MacLeod, M. A., Robinson, M., MacKay, J., & Dobinson, C. (2014). Mental Health and substance use among bisexual youth and non-youth in Ontario, Canada. *PLOS One, 9*(8). doi:10.1371/journal.pone.0101604

Ross, L. E, O'Gorman, L., MacLeod, M. A., Bauer, G. R., MacKay, J., & Robinson, M. (2016). Bisexuality, poverty, and mental health: A mixed methods analysis. *Social Science & Medicine, 156*, 64–72. doi:http://dx.doi.org/10.1016/j.socscimed.2016.03.009

Rust, P. C. (1995). Bisexuality and the challenge to lesbian politics: Sex, loyalty, and revolution. New York, NY: NYU Press.

Scheim, A., Jackson, R., James, L., Sharp Dopler, T., Pyne, J., & Bauer, G. R. (2013). Barriers to well-being for Aboriginal gender-diverse people: Results from the Trans PULSE project in Ontario, Canada. *Ethnicity and Inequalities in Health and Social Care, 6*(4), 108–120. http://dx.doi.org/10.1108/EIHSC-08-2013-0010

Simoni, J. M., Walters, K. L., Balsam, K. F., & Meyers, S. B. (2006). Victimization, substance use, and HIV risk behaviors among gay/bisexual/two-spirit and heterosexual American Indian men in New York City. *American Journal of Public Health, 96*(12), 2240–2245. doi:10.2105/AJPH.2004.054056

Smith, A. (2005). *Conquest: Sexual violence and American Indian genocide*. Cambridge, MA: South End Press.

Smith, A. (2010). Queer theory and Native studies: the heteronormativity of settler colonialism. *GLQ: A Journal of Lesbian and Gay Studies, 16*(1.2), 41–68. doi:10.1215/10642684-2009-012

Storr, M. (Ed.). (2013). *Bisexuality: A critical reader*. New York, NY: Routledge.

Suresha, R., & Chavny, P. (2006). *Bi Men: Coming out every which way*. New York, NY: Harrington Park Press.

Taylor, C., Peter, T., McMinn, T. L., Elliott, T., Beldom, S., Ferry, A., ... Schachter, K. (2011). *Every class in every school: The first national climate survey on homophobia, biphobia, and transphobia in Canadian schools. Final report.* Toronto, Canada: Egale Canada Human Rights Trust. Retrieved from http://egale.ca/youth-and-safer-schools/national-survey/every-class/

Tsai, W. H. S. (2010). Assimilating the queers: Representations of lesbians, gay men, bisexual, and transgender people in mainstream advertising. *Advertising & Society Review, 11*(1), doi:10.1353/asr.0.0042

Tucker, N., Highleyman, L., & Kaplan, R. (1995). *Bisexual politics: Theories, queries & visions.* New York, NY: Harrington Park Press.

Walters, M. L., Chen, J., & Breiding, M. J. (2013). *The National Intimate Partner and Sexual Violence Survey (NISVS): 2010 findings on victimization by sexual orientation.* Atlanta, GA: Centers for Disease Control and Prevention, National Center for Injury Prevention and Control. Retrieved from http://www.cdc.gov/violenceprevention/pdf/nisvs_sofindings.pdf

Wilson, A. (2008). N'tacinowin inna nah': Our coming in stories. *Canadian Woman Studies, 26*(3), 193–199.

Home-o: Being at Home with Reflections on Hetero-Homosexual Identity

Joshua Nash

ABSTRACT
This article presents a creative interpretation of interaction between hetero- and homosexual worlds. The metaphor of home is used to transfer different meanings and experiences of hetero-homosexuality into private and personal takes on bisexuality and being heteroflexible. Self-knowledge is implicitly equated with awareness of one's sexuality.

How can heterosexual male experiences and musings be used to interpret the state of being under the bisexual umbrella? Is being bicurious really a state of bisexuality or simply a transient and possibly mobile sexual condition? Can a creative interpretation of hetero-homosexual contact offer anything to theoretical understandings of a diversity of sexual experiences and makeups within the exploratory sexual world of middle-class men in their late twenties? Although the present deliberation will go far from conclusively answering any of these questions, the experimental writing and its force of expression is offered as a means to reconcile certain elements of male sexuality within the realm of a perception of late modern male sexual identity.

There is a mass of literature to consult relating bisexuality, hetero-bicuriosity, and sexual identity theory and its role within plural sexuality. Here I restrict my review to that which is conducive to inventive formulation, injecting the personal into the writing of what can be considered investigational (bi)sexual and hetero-homosexual involvement. Barker's (2006) short and punchy statements about why we should at all study the emplacement of bisexual studies go some way to forming the intellectual repository as to the wherefore of dipping into bisexual identities. Here it is really the 'beyond' of Barker's 'bisexuality and beyond' that seizes and begins the apparent need to 'resist the binary' (e.g., Bowes-Catton, 2007) when pointing toward bisexual identities. Is bicuriosity actually anything clearly demarcated or something less menacing, nothing really to worry about, a more transient and just an overly volatile setting open to unpredictability, erraticism, and change?

Bridges' (2014) 'a very "gay" straight' would have us believe in fuzzy boundaries and layers of complexity which may be crossed, with the results depending entirely on reasoning, emotion, and even total loss of sexual compass. Within this ambit, Allison and Risman's (2014) 'hooking up' or sexual activity outside relationships is brought to bear on the hetero- and homosexual playing field, together in the real world and distinct in the character privy arena.

I intend my short treatise to add incrementally to this theoretical backdrop. The setting is entirely city-based: Copenhagen, Denmark, early winter 2002. The topic: the impermanence of urban relationships in two males' late twenties. The hetero is the author, the chased, Australian. The other, the chaser, the homo[1], from the Caribbean. We are both outsiders in this dark and wintery land.

The beginning of being homeward bound

So there he stood. By the door, the one at the front of my home. Looking tall, gay, handsome. I couldn't and still cannot fathom it. His name, a pseudonym, is Felix Ferdinand, and he said he loves me. I am shocked though not surprised in the least. He tempted me. I saw and felt an intention from his side that I know I have felt for my preference, the female, the softer ones, those with whom I have been before. In the eyes. The movement of the body. His body. The sigh. You know, the dropping of the breath when you know it counts. The eyes of several others have done the same. But this time he is shyer. He made a pass, but we never went through with anything. I like girls. I keep telling him so. I like girls. He doesn't want to believe me. He keeps trying. We continue our discussion. I like girls.

I have two homes. One is my work and the other my home. I have started to refer to the latter as my home-o, or hom-e-o, because of the homo who is often home with me. I spend much time at both homes. One gives money whereas the other gives rest and realization and occasionally a gay man to visit. This is what my piece is all about.

The singularity and plurality of my home and my homos.[2] There is more to this than sex. Why? It's because the sex will never happen. I will never go with him. What is this 'go'? Is it just sex or something much deeper? Is 'to go with him' doing what I am now doing? I will be seeing Felix on Tuesday night. We'll observe pictures at an exhibition. We're meeting at a gallery. Felix's 'him,' the soon to be ex-husband, will apparently be there. He (Felix) doesn't really want to be with him (the soon to be ex), but they still live together and are married. He's French. There is some Romance language–based connection in all of this. An undercurrent of an unknown inspiration toward something involving my emerging bicuriosity. I really don't want to break up anyone's marriage.

Maybe I'd work in the Copenhagen gay scene. Would I prefer to be liked in the hetero scene, if there even exists such a stage? A woman that picks me out and says 'it's you I want.' Maybe I'd be scared if it happened right now. No, I want to be raped. But not by him. Mentally he's already done it. This I wasn't scared of. It's the other element I query. The physical. The emotions are nothing to be scared of. I've felt that in another homo, the Australian one. Still, my only real home-o is here with my connections and the things I know and understand so well in my home. It could well be interaction and 'sex between straight white men,' in the true sense of being not gay (Ward, 2015) if you ask me. For all I care. But it's not, there's something else occurring.

The girls are the ones who make me flutter inside. But I have been tempted in the other direction. As in, I am right now. He tempts and I back off. This is more my style. Curious but not serious. I could take some chances, but I think they might scare me. I'd be scared off, into something I never knew, will never know, and perhaps was never destined to know. I am only thinking of the sex. There can't be anything else, because the else is a lead into that. You know, the inevitable. It's bound to happen. The gay man's brain I know. It's like like attracting like or the opposite sides of a pole. There is that air of the heart beating at least. Home is where the heart is. I may have found mine. A home with a homo. The evolving home-o. Whether she, he, or I are sure is still to be ascertained. I know the feeling now, though. For me it's about touchy feely. That 'oooh' feeling once she said. I've become overwhelmed again. Five minutes ago a colleague told me on the phone, "*Du er lige ved at blive en mand*" (you are about to become a man). This meant a lot to me. Looking for the definition of a man has been a big part of my spiritual and sexual quest. And I asked many in this regard about what they thought it meant to be manlike, sexually mature, to possess prowess. I am not sure if this has anything to do with home-o. It's the homo I am at home with, a part of and the Self inside. The book I am at home with. The publishing of something not to be described in words but done so to produce something. A description of a home base. An underlay. An underlying sensuality and sexuality entitled only to those who are tracking such a thing. I've been told I am a candidate. It is somehow showing. Like the boys. The gay Australian thinks I am getting more than he is at present. I don't want them. But then I do. I'll make a move on him one day. He'll just have to wait and see. Am I moving from the typical 'strong and silent' heterosexual (Sender, 2006) through metrosexuality and bicurious to another new moniker to me, the "heteroflexible" (Hubbard, 2008)?

This place where I live is my current home. The city, yeah, I've written about it all before. I also ring the Caribbean homo. It's strange that he doesn't feel at home here, yet he still persists in being and living so. I know the limitations of being here: time, love, a citizen of here I'll never be. The guys are still looked at, and I, too, feel their eyes. Just leading them on. I just know that if I kissed him it wouldn't stop there. Or just sleeping in his bed holding hands. My hands go sweaty and clammy at the thought(s). They do say curiosity killed the cat, so this keeps me back. Makes me write about the boys and not feel them. Have them in my dreams and not in my bed. Imagination and not my pillow. Being with a girl is like running down a hill. Being with a man like running up.

I have seen two lesbian pairs in the last 2 days. I thought of home-o and what it may mean. Where Felix and I might be a pretty boy crossover, they could be a pretty girl something-or-other. I doubt they would like me. Being quite feminine and all. They might eat me for dinner. But what is it they do? How is it they love? I 'can' love a man, I think, I am feeling it, but it has little to do with sex or being intimate. I am realizing how important this time is: for opening up, meeting the right people, staring, and leading guys on. Sometimes I think it should be two hetero guys together, not a duo of one and the other. Two heteroflexibles maybe. A monotomy among a dichotomy. Is it a hetero identity plus a descript sexual adventuring beyond the boundaries of my 'straightness' (Albury, 2015)?

Two heteroflexibles could lie in bed and say the same things rather than thinking that the other is thinking differently. I've seen some of these guys. They might even be my friends. To sleep in the same bed together. The process and how it is we get there. Is it through intimacy or a selfish confidence in the s/Self? Sleeping with as many as you can? There's no one knocking on my door tonight, and I'm glad. I think I'd maybe even deny them. That tiredness inside and a wanting of being alone. And its difference from not being lonely. Warm smiles and keeping him preciously inside.

I'm home inside where the warmth is snug and the ideals of casual sex meeting a romantic nonsexual encounter with a gay male (cf. Reay, 2014) seem so much more likely than anything 'hetero-' (other, different).

Absence, developing, trying

Felix has been absent from my life of late. It was Tuesday (this is October 2002) we last saw each other. He was late, but it wasn't raining. The leaves were falling off the trees. They still are. He can sing. I know. It is a part of the whole show. The hetero among several gay boys. One in Denmark, the other one written to in Australia. I am the meat in the sandwich. They seem to believe I taste good. I was in Sweden yesterday and thought of how Swedish guys must be. Probably harder for me to talk to them and they'd use names like Göran and Olaf. Plus that song I wrote about them in 1998 with the line: 'Conservatism, high drinking age, safe cars, and men called Sven.' The people on the other side of The Sound, Øresund, the body of water between Denmark and Sweden. The bridge, that connection. There's no place like home. Returning to my quarters somehow scares me and makes me feel alienated. It's like I have lived too long within hetero-quartered domains. In his absence, I feel a development, some change. Sexual flexibility.

I know it's just a stage. I'll get over it. Being on his side of the fence. Talking, thinking, and writing camp when deep down I am everything but. Everything but the boy. Everything but the sex with which I am trying to tackle and understand, a type of heteronormativity-cum-sexual secrecy (Cassar, 2015). The safe domicile, sometimes together, sometimes apart. The Scandinavian lighting makes an important contribution to my home. The lamps from this part of the world are for use in this part of the world. I have taken photos in my apartment. It's where I reside. One couldn't see the bed, however. And besides, I'm the only guy who's slept there. More than one girl has sat there, but I dare not write about them in my current company. The boys in the home are what matter. In my heart and at a distance. The desire to travel seems not to go away. I think of the transformative power of the mobility I experience and its sexualized means. Hetero-metro-flexible.

He tried again last night. It was just the same, but this time a little more forcefully executed. I was not impressed, but I didn't flinch. There was something there on my side, but I cannot understand what this was other than sexual frustration. Force might not ever work. Us interrupting each other while talking made me think this was not the right consciousness to be in. Two lines going parallel. Not meeting. So how could we even meet physically? I may want one thing and he could possibly give it to me.

But he wants something that I cannot or do not want to offer. Here home-o (also said like 'cameo') has come to a painful reality. So I may still think and ask of friendship and its place among feelings of sex (his side) and noncomplacency (my side). To quote De La Soul, *Stakes is High* (Mercer et al., 1996), "Welcome to reality, see times is hard."

We danced to house music and I did feel something for him. I think I even wanted to flirt. Oh no, what am I thinking? Am I becoming gay from this writing? I have written camp many times to other gay friends, but this is something novel, unmapped. An even testing of myself to see whether I, too, will fall for the trap I myself have placed before myself. Myself and himself. You, the reader, hearing my thoughts about the same sex while not having sex with anyone. I am thinking to give up and let it flow.

That amazing feeling can and will be had again (with a woman), but it is the patience that needs to wait. I mean, the patience that will help me wait.

The world knows what I want and it isn't a man, any man, however saucy he may be, however strong he may appear. I may want to admire him at a distance, but he'll never sleep in my bed. Not for any money or any pain or even sensuality. This relationship is making me want to open up to something I have found deep within myself. And it is real, hetero and based in the home. Inside is where the happiness is.

Metrovert het(e)rovert extrovert, *Xtro*. The underground (metro) of the city of Copenhagen has recently been opened, I am more or less hetero, and *Xtro* was a horror flick from the 1980s. I will go to the underground in the near future, but to expend energy and the money for such a purpose eludes my intellect. Anyway, back to the story. The homo hasn't been in my home-o for some time now. But I like his company and his absence, too. Especially that of last meeting. A cozy café, an understanding, a speaking. Some fluency in communication. Dark nights getting cold.

(I feel like using the word 'complacency' here. Done.) He is looking for an external Paris, but it is inside him the real Paris exists. Copenhagen is the Paris of the north. I will write about this. Perhaps in a song for one of the boys. Somehow he deserves it. A blending of homes, life, and sexual preferences. Maybe I'm already over my head. With the man, the one with whom I spend nights after short days. We make music in the life we are now leading and of which we are becoming a part. He's a homo, and our home-o is becoming something much more than real. He's more than a friend. Yes, the invitation to create a new world, our home, our campness in conversation and existence and accepting things as they are. The honesty and a giving of much more than one receives. And the current realization being a manifestation of the Greek basis for the root *homo-*. All this side knows is that one meaning is 'same.' It's a worry. Not a life, the life, the music or the home. No, the worry is that the guy is becoming a part of this discourse. He was the inspiration, oh yes: a mode and means of behavior, the male in the dark, the come-ons and our meetings after work. He's mentally and intellectually fulfilled my needs of the last 2 months. And the sexual? Well, he has tried and I took a step back. More than once and both times in my home. My home soil with the dim lights on and the candles slowly burning down. There was a smell of incense in the room and the autumn shadow had already come. Cold rain. There also must have been dinner at some stage and the smell of spices in the air. It all led to his action and my withdrawal. And with this time it was real as the action was there and it was not just a matter of fantasy and belief. He wanted to find out what it is about. My being and even my soul.

Am I becoming a 'feminised male' (cf. Craine & Aitken, 2004)? Can you keep a secret? The boy is in the home again. I hear music of my distant other gay friends and think of the colors fading, the arrows through my heart, and the twentysomething fan club established for and around the tabernacle of the boys at home.

The depth of relationships with the man can be so much more fulfilling. Even knowing where the gaps are and being able to fill them in a/the proper way.

It's him I sit with in Copenhagen's cafés while the girls look on not knowing what quantity they're observing. They think we're already taken, and thus they flirt but still look on with the occasional interested glance. Somehow my attention is drawn away though I should be looking in their direction. It's because the science he studies and lives and the way his mind works are apparently more than I'll find in the realm of such a situation and place. Ok, the dim candles glow and the smell of perfume, alcohol, and cigarettes permeate an atmosphere I've seen so many times before. Girls with dead foxes around their necks pose an offer that I oftentimes find so hard to read, although the opportunity to read between the lines in 'abnormal situations' is more beneficial for these eyes. Denmark can restrict. I will soon be gone. I doubt he ever wants to go back to the Caribbean.

Judging from the cold outside it could be Paris or Berlin, but the heart here is where my home is. And the gayness makes for gaiety deep inside. There is a true warmth there and a spontaneity. No calendars, no 'I've got no time'—it's either 'I've got time' so we then meet or 'I've got no time—we'll meet tomorrow'. Assurance, guarantees, we'll definitely meet soon. His past mate is moving away again soon. The ex-husband. This side will also move and not be there for him. The distant city sleeping and knowing what he's thinking will make it all worthwhile. When I leave, we will together be occupants in my backpack and my heart. They don't need physical space, merely a wish and a desire for being together with me, my home, my posse, my idea(l)s, my pen, my paper, my life as music, my life as art and as building. The breeze is stiffening and almost all the leaves are gone. My upper lip is becoming softer instead of harder, and living is becoming milder and directed in the right direction.

The homos moving about in my life are a justified condition/conclusion of this softening. They're giving me more than I can give them right now. Still present is the smell of incense and spices. At home waiting for the homo. Again, that hetero feeling.

Change, progression, summary

I was at home with a girl. A Norwegian on Christianshavn. There was the thought of whether she wanted me. The way she looked into my eyes told a story. Her bed looked comfortable though expectations can be dangerous things. There was some contact, but my tiredness killed anything in the end. Asleep in her bed might have made some difference, but this was never to be. She made me feel hetero once more. I never stayed and went home to my home-o. And I never saw her again. Many people have told me I am too intense.

My home here is clean, the floor white, space, a feeling of leaving and a missing of the country I am still in. When I next travel, this is where I'll be missing/I'll be missing, nowhere else (Nash & Gorman-Murray, 2014). Always the people, always the sun. The people, the guy, the nakedness, the reason to be, things are not becoming any easier. It's dangerous to establish things that cannot be finished, leaving a heart in a place one will not see for up to 6 months. I soon leave for the subcontinent, a place of much concealed homosexuality (e.g., Vanita, 2002). It begins to hurt now as the days are nearly not days and the cold has more than crept in. The appreciation has to come, is still to come.

It's all coming closer to home. He's looking for the homerun, and it seems the batter's up in this home. But I cannot explicate more than any reader might be able to take. It's hurting me so much. Inside and out. I don't know what's come of me. A home and a homo at this place, topos, scene, and time. It's like the *Blair Witch Project*—it ends before we know what happens. But the real story has been told. I'm at home with a homo.

Applying Flanders, Dobinson, and Logie's (2015) phrase "I'm never really my full self" of women's perceptions of their mental health to my own querying of the heteronormality-cum-heteronormativity of my own sexuality in general and the diversity of autoexperience and identity application, it appears the equation home + homo = home-o is appropriate to liken a specific recollection of being at home, being at peace, with hetero-homosexual identity. The 'home' is key: it is a location and locator of normativity, a place which creates norms, sexually and thought wise.

Here the home and the safe space in interaction with a person becoming a friend and eventual lover and even coresearcher meld to establish the home expanse as a fruitful geography for hetero-homo-normativity (cf. Hubbard, 2008). It is possible that questioning the lived reality of bicuriosity and the apparently benign and private engagement in hetero-homo acts of a bisexuality reaching for a more developed plurisexuality, particularly in the domain of home can reveal much of how modern sexual intersection might occur. Heteroflexiblity and homoflexiblity now appear as two more settled possibilities within and under the bisexual umbrella.

Acknowledgment

I express my gratitude to the two gay men—'Felix' and 'the gay Australian'—whose presence was integral to the writing of this piece.

Notes

1. As regards the use of the noun 'homo,' I am aware of the historical stigma around the term and its use. I do not in any way use 'homo' in a derogatory sense. On the contrary, I use it throughout almost as a 'homely' and 'home-based' term of endearment, as a way to bridge gaps between the sexualities I discuss. 'My homo' can almost be equated with 'my dear.' In addition, the word play involving 'homo' and the title of this piece 'Home-o' (pronounceable as 'home-o' and 'hom-e-o') partially necessitates the inclusion and use of 'homo' to make sense of the sexual and home focused context of the piece.
2. It is essential to explain the use of the singular and the plural: homo and homos. Although I am writing about interaction with one particular gay man and how my heterosexuality has been challenged and questioned greatly by our interaction, the original unpublished piece 'Home-o' written in Copenhagen, Denmark in October 2002 was presented primarily as a letter-cum-diary-cum-journal to a male gay friend and artistic collaborator in Australia. In this sense, I often move freely between the singular and plural and speaking to 'my homo' or 'my homos.'

References

Albury, K. (2015). Identity plus? Bi-curiosity, sexual adventurism and the boundaries of 'straight' sexual practices and identities. *Sexualities, 18*(5/6), 649–664.

Allison, R., & Risman, B. J. (2014). "It goes hand in hand with the parties": Race, class, and residence in college student negotiations of hooking up. *Sociological Perspectives, 57*(1), 102–123.

Barker, M. (2006). Why I study … Bisexuality and beyond. *The Psychologist, 19*(1), 33–34.

Bowes-Catton, H. (2007). Resisting the binary: Discourses of identity and diversity in bisexual politics 1988-1996. *Lesbian & Gay Psychology Review*, *8*(1), 58–70.

Bridges, T. (2014). A very "gay" straight? Hybrid masculinities, sexual aesthetics, and the changing relationship between masculinity and homophobia. *Gender & Society*, *28*(1), 58–82.

Cassar, J. (2015). Sex and secrecies: An exploration of students' conceptualizations of heteronormativity. *Journal of LGBT Youth*, *12*(4), 419–435.

Craine, J., & Aitken, S. (2004). Street fighting: Placing the crisis of masculinity in David Fincher's *Fight Club*. *Geojournal*, *59*, 289–296.

Flanders, C. E., Dobinson, C., & Logie, C. (2015). "I'm never really my full self": Young bisexual women's perceptions of their mental health. *Journal of Bisexuality*, *15*(4), 454–480.

Hubbard, P. (2008). Here, There, Everywhere: The Ubiquitous Geographies of Heteronormativity. *Geography Compass*, *2/3*(2008), 640–658.

Mercer, K., Jolicoeur, D., Mason, V., & Yancey, J. (1996). Stakes Is High [Recorded by De La Soul]. On *Stakes Is High* [CD]. New York, NY: Tommy Boy Records.

Nash, C. J., & Gorman-Murray, A. (2014). LGBT neighbourhoods and 'new mobilities': Towards understanding transformations in sexual and gendered urban landscapes. *International Journal of Urban and Regional Research*, *38*(3), 756–772.

Reay, B. (2014). Promiscuous intimacies: Rethinking the history of American casual sex. *Journal of Historical Sociology*, *27*(1), 1–24.

Sender, K. (2006). Queens for a day: Queer eye for the straight guy and the neoliberal project. *Critical Studies in Media Communication*, *23*, 131–151.

Vanita, R. (2002). *Queering India: Same-sex love and eroticism in Indian culture and society*. New York, NY: Routledge.

Ward, J. (2015). *Not gay: Sex between straight white men*. New York, NY: New York University Press.

Defining Bisexuality: Young Bisexual and Pansexual People's Voices

Corey E. Flanders, Marianne E. LeBreton, Margaret Robinson, Jing Bian, and Jaime Alonso Caravaca-Morera

ABSTRACT
Bisexuality is defined in a plethora of ways, including definitions based on behavior, attraction, or desire and may employ binary or nonbinary definitions. Research has not adequately addressed how young bisexual people themselves define bisexuality, whether those definitions change with social context, or whether bisexual people define bisexuality differently from pansexual people. The current study addresses these questions through an online, mixed-methods study. A total of 60 bisexual and pansexual participants aged ages 18 to 30 responded to closed- and open-ended questions regarding their definitions of bisexuality. Closed-ended responses were analyzed with a series of chi-square tests, while we conducted a summative content analysis on the open-ended responses. Results indicate that in general, bisexual and pansexual people define bisexuality similarly. Participants modified their definitions of bisexuality depending upon the social context. Implications for research are discussed.

Introduction

Although many researchers have written on the topic of defining bisexuality (e.g., Barker, Bowes-Catton, Iantaffi, Cassidy, & Brewer, 2008; Bauer & Brennan, 2013; Galupo, 2011), relatively less research has explored how young bisexual people define their sexuality. Further, research has not adequately addressed how definitions may vary given social context. For example, how people define bisexuality for themselves may differ from definitions shared with others, or people with other plurisexual identities, like pansexual people, may define bisexuality differently than do bisexual people. The current study aims to explore these questions by investigating how bisexuality is conceptualized across different scenarios by people ages 18 to 30 who self-identify as bisexual and pansexual, all of whom felt the label of bisexuality applied to them.

Defining bisexuality

Researchers define bisexuality in a multitude of ways, often depending upon the particular research questions involved in a given study. We discuss defining bisexuality as an "umbrella term," as a behavior, as a self-identity, and as a binary or nonbinary identity. In each section, we also discuss associated research implications of each definitional practice.

The bisexual umbrella

Researchers often theorize bisexuality as the midpoint between heterosexuality and homosexuality. This practice places less of an emphasis on bisexuality as an independent identity and more on how it exists relative to monosexualities (i.e., identities that refer to attraction to just one sex and/or gender). Defining bisexuality in a relative context facilitates combining it with other nonmonosexual identities as the focus is not on particular identities but rather the category of nonmonosexuality. This grouping of nonmonosexual people and identities is what is often described as the "bisexual umbrella."

Due to sample size, research literature rarely distinguishes between bisexuality and other nonmonosexual identities, such as pansexuality, fluid sexuality, or omnisexuality, and instead utilizes the umbrella approach, combining nonmonosexual identities into one category recoded as "bisexual" (Callis, 2014; Mitchell, Davis, & Galupo, 2014; Rust, 2001). Using this practice better enables researchers to garner samples large enough to assess important issues that may impact nonmonosexual people as a whole, like health inequities. However, it may also serve to falsely categorize people as bisexual and erase important differences between people who identify as bisexual and those who do not (Persson & Pfaus, 2015). For instance, pansexual people are generally grouped under the bisexual umbrella but have been found to report different experiences of stigma within queer community than those reported by bisexual people (Mitchell et al., 2014).

Bisexuality defined by behavior, attraction, and desire

Researchers also use bisexuality as an umbrella term to describe a wide range of sexual behaviors, attractions, and desires. Some researchers have gone as far as specifying sexual or relationship behavior with more than one gender as criteria for being included as bisexual participants (Rosenthal, Sylva, Safron, & Bailey, 2011). However, defining bisexuality based on behavior may not reflect the experiences of bisexual people.

Considering young people, recent research indicates that more young people are identifying as a sexual minority person prior to first sexual activity (Morgan, 2011).

In addition, research with young bisexual women indicates that the pressure to define one's sexual identity based upon sexual or relationship history may have adverse sexual and mental health consequences (Flanders, Dobinson, & Logie, 2016). Thus, people who identify under the bisexual umbrella may not endorse particular behavioral criteria as essential to identifying as bisexual.

Bauer and colleagues have called for researchers to acknowledge that behavior is not interchangeable with identity, and that the way in which researchers conceptualize sexual orientation will impact their results (Bauer & Brennan, 2013; Bauer & Jairam, 2008). Bauer and Jairam (2008) classified the same pool of women by sexual identity, and by two measures of behavior (sex of past-year partners, and sex of lifetime partners) and found that health outcomes differed significantly depending on how sexuality was categorized. Although behavior may be an important criterion to consider for some research questions, it is not sufficient on its own to fully understand health issues associated with bisexuality.

Bisexual umbrella identities as binary and nonbinary

In addition to variations in how bisexuality is conceptualized within research, identities under the bisexual umbrella may also differ in terms of how they are defined socially. Jakubowski (2014) describes pansexual identity, for example, as intentionally prioritizing "romantic and/or sexual attractions to genderqueer, agender, and other nonbinary people and politics." Some, such as Albo (2015), have contrasted pansexual identity with bisexuality, defining the latter as referring only "to people liking both men and women," and as not including "a wider variety of gender-neutral or gender-fluid terminology." However, though these definitions place pansexuality and bisexuality as distinct from one another with pansexuality as nonbinary (encompassing attraction to a range of genders) and bisexuality as binary (encompassing attraction to only men and women), this may not reflect how many bisexual people themselves define bisexuality.

The current study sheds light on whether such distinctions are relevant to bisexual and pansexual people who self-identify under the bisexual umbrella. Although a desire to be gender inclusive may certainly influence sexual identity label choice, there may also be social factors, such as age, racialization, or class, involved in determining which labels are accessible or useful to particular individuals. Further, the label people use may depend upon social context, in that sometimes participants may use bisexual if they feel it is more accessible in a situation in contrast to pansexual (McAllum, 2015). This article places a focus on age, as recent research indicates young people approach sexual identity labels in ways that diverge from previous generations (Coleman-Fountain, 2014).

Considering research implications, it is possible that if researchers define bisexuality as a binary attraction to men and women, they risk excluding people who identify as bisexual but experience attraction to more than two genders, and thus collecting nonrepresentative data. Further, many people who identify as bisexual also identify with another nonmonosexual identity, including pansexuality, which blurs the line of distinction between these identities (Bauer, Flanders, MacLeod, & Ross, 2016). Recent research with bisexual populations indicates that those who identity as bisexual only may represent a distinct group in terms of health outcomes compared with those who identify as bisexual in addition to other labels such as pansexual or queer (Bauer et al., 2016).

The current study

As research findings can vary depending upon how bisexuality is defined, it is important to understand whether, how, and when definitions used by researchers align with how bisexual people themselves define their identity to know how accurately bisexual research reflects the lived realities of bisexual people. The current study provides information on how participants who self-identify under the bisexual umbrella, either as bisexual or pansexual, define bisexuality. This includes how they define bisexuality for themselves and others, and whether they view any specific attractions or behaviors as necessary for bisexual identity.

We used closed- and open-ended questions to collect participants' definitions; the quantitative responses allow for clear comparisons across groups, and qualitative data contextualize participants' responses. Further, using qualitative methods facilitates the inclusion of participants' voices, which is particularly important for groups that have been historically marginalized and pathologized in research. Although this study is predominantly qualitative and thus should not be generalized beyond our sample, this work may inform the understanding of ways in which bisexuality can be defined, particularly in research conducted with young bisexual and other plurisexual people.

Method

Ethical approval was obtained from the University of Hawaii. This study used a subset of data from a parent study that investigated daily experiences of young bisexual people's daily experiences related to their sexual identity and well-being (Flanders, 2015). As a component of this research, participants responded to questions about their definitions of bisexuality, and those data are examined here.

Sample

Participants were recruited by convenience sampling at the University of Hawaii, as well as through social media platforms and listservs. Inclusion criteria required participants to (1) be between ages 18 and 30, (2) be able to read and write in English, (3) have Internet access, and (4) identify as bisexual or feel the label of bisexual applied to them. A total of 91 participants were recruited for the parent study, 60 of whom are included in the current subset of data. Participants were excluded from the present analysis if they did not respond to the questions attended to in this analysis, or if they did not explicitly identify as either bisexual or pansexual. The number of participants identifying with other labels, such as queer, was too few to conduct meaningful comparisons across groups. Although inclusion criteria mandated that people identified as bisexual or felt the label of bisexuality applied to them, after accessing the online survey participants were asked to select a single sexual identity from a list that also included a write-in option. Forty-nine participants identified as bisexual, and 11 identified as pansexual. Participant ages ranged from 18 to 30, with an average of 22.98 ($SD =$ 3.49), with pansexual participants being significantly older than bisexual participants, $F(1,58) = 9.52$, $p = .003$. A total of 20 participants identified as male, 32 as female, seven as genderqueer, and one person chose not to disclose their gender identity. Forty-five participants identified as White, 14 as people of color, and one person chose not to disclose.

Data collection

People who expressed interest in the study were e-mailed a link to the survey. Upon accessing the link, participants were given an informed consent form. If they consented to participate, they were automatically routed to the online survey. After completing the survey, participants had the option of requesting a $15 Amazon.com gift card as compensation. All links between participant e-mail addresses and survey data were destroyed.

Measures

The current analysis examines open-ended and closed-ended questions asking how participants defined bisexuality, as well as a brief demographic form. Open-ended questions included (1) In general, how would you define bisexuality? (2) What does being bisexual mean to you personally? (3) How would you describe your bisexual identity to someone else? (4) What type of behaviors does a person need to exhibit in order to be bisexual, if any? and (5) What type of desires does a person need to exhibit in order to be bisexual, if any?

In the closed-ended portion, participants responded 'yes' or 'no' to whether they endorsed the following statements to be accurate definitions of bisexuality: (1) Someone who is romantically interested in two or more genders, (2) Someone who is sexually interested in two or more genders, (3) Someone who has had romantic relationships with people of two or more genders, (4) Someone who has had sexual relationships with two or more genders, (5) Someone who has the capacity for romantic interest in two or more genders, and (6) Someone who has the capacity for sexual interest in two or more genders.

Data analysis

We analyzed responses to the open-ended questions using a summative qualitative content analysis approach (Hsieh & Shannon, 2005), in which words and related content are identified in terms of their frequency of use and their contextual meaning. Four of the authors open coded each of the participant responses to develop potential codes. After the initial open coding, we discussed our respective codes and developed a unified coding framework, which was integrated into a table with a row for each code and a column for each participant. This coding framework can be found in the appendix. We then recoded all of the data, indicating which codes were identified in each participant's responses. All participant responses were coded by two of the authors independently, and then each coding pair met to discuss any discrepancies until there was a consensus for each of the codes. These data were transposed and uploaded to SPSS version 21 to generate frequencies for each code. In addition, we conducted chi-square analyses to compare the responses of bisexual participants to those of pansexual participants, as well as to compare responses across questions (e.g., to determine whether responses differed significantly in the first question compared to the second question). We also performed chi-square analyses with the closed-ended responses to compare the responses of bisexual and pansexual participants.

Results

Closed-ended responses

The frequencies for each of the closed-ended question responses can be found in Table 1. Most participants endorsed statements describing bisexual identity as sexual or romantic interest in two or more genders, or as having the capacity for sexual or romantic interest in two or more genders. Most participants did not endorse the statements that indicated people must have engaged in sexual or romantic relationships with people of two or more genders to be bisexual, which is in line with the content analysis findings. There were no significant differences between the responses of bisexual and pansexual participants, though the generalizability of

Table 1. Frequencies for the close-ended question responses on bisexual identity.

Question	Identity	Responded Yes[a]	χ^2	p	r
Romantically interested in two or more genders	Bisexual	42	0.107	0.744	0.04
	Pansexual	9			
Sexually interested in two or more genders	Bisexual	42	0.107	0.744	0.04
	Pansexual	9			
Romantic Relationships with two or more genders	Bisexual	29	0.080	0.778	0.04
	Pansexual	5			
Sexual Relationships with two or more genders	Bisexual	15	0.137	0.711	0.05
	Pansexual	4			
Capacity for romantic interest in two or more genders	Bisexual	42	1.779	0.182	0.17
	Pansexual	11			
Capacity for sexual interest in two or more genders	Bisexual	41	2.072	0.150	0.19
	Pansexual	11			

Note.
[a]For the column "Responded Yes" the number is out of 60 participants.

these findings is limited by the small sample of participants who identified as pansexual.

Content analysis

The primary categories identified for Questions 1 through 3 (general definition of bisexuality; what being bisexual means to people personally; and describing bisexuality to someone else) are attraction, gender, and fluidity. Secondary codes (those occurring frequently but not present across all questions) included self-identification and stigma. Qualities necessary for bisexual identity were explored in Questions 4 and 5, which asked about the behavior and desires required to be bisexual, if any. Although we compare the responses of pansexual and bisexual participants, it is important to note that as these data are qualitative, they are not generalizable beyond our sample. Further, the interpretation of findings should be contextualized within the limitation of the small sample of pansexual people relative to those who identified as bisexual.

Attraction

Many participants wrote about attraction in their open-ended responses. Some used general descriptions of attraction, meaning they did not expand upon type of attraction, such as sexual or romantic, in their descriptions of bisexuality. One participant (female, bisexual), for example, stated "[b]eing attracted to more than one sex." This type of description was open to interpretation as to what type of attraction participants were referring.

Others specified sexual, romantic, physical, and/or emotional attraction. When specified, it was more common for participants to write that bisexuality includes one or more types of attraction (indicated with the disjunctive "or") whereas a smaller proportion of participants specified more than one form of attraction was necessary (indicated with the conjunctive "and"). For example, one participant (male, pansexual) defined bisexuality as "[a]ttraction, both sexual and romantic to more than one sex," whereas another (female, bisexual) stated, "[b]isexuality to me is being attracted (romantically or sexually) to people of both sexes (male and female)." Listing possible attractions indicates a flexibility in definition; one need not, for example, feel sexual and romantic attraction toward more than one gender are necessary to be bisexual, but rather one or the other would be sufficient.

In comparing bisexual and pansexual participant responses, the only significant relationship between sexual identity and how attraction was discussed was in Question 1. In this case, fewer bisexual people than expected (44.90%) and more pansexual people than expected (81.82%) included sexual attraction in their definition of bisexuality, $\chi^2 = 4.90, p = .027, r = .29$. This indicates that among our participants, sexual attraction is a more salient aspect of bisexual identity for pansexual people than for bisexual people.

Comparing responses across questions, sexual attraction was more likely to be endorsed when defining bisexuality generally than in describing what being bisexual meant to participants personally ($\chi^2 = 9.025$, $p = .003$, $r = .39$), or in describing their bisexual identity to someone else ($\chi^2 = 18.15$, $p < .01$, $r = .55$). For our participants, this indicates that sexual attraction may be more salient as a general aspect of bisexuality, whereas it may be less salient or relevant to what being bisexual means to them personally or as a way to describe their identity to others.

Gender

Participants used a wide range of language to talk about gender and/or sex. For example, people used "gender" and "sex" in their responses, as well as phrases such as "men and women" or "boys and girls." One participant wrote, "Bisexuality is when someone feels romantic and physical attraction to both sexes" (female, bisexual), compared to another who described bisexuality as "Being attracted to or loving both genders" (female, bisexual). Although it is possible participants who used the terminology of sex and terms that are associated with sex, like "male," "female," and "intersex," meant something different than those who used gender and terms such as "men," "women," and "trans," we are not able to discern whether that is the case based on these data.

In general, references to gender and/or sex were used to describe bisexuality as attraction to more than one gender or sex. However, other participants reported that gender, sex, or in some instances, genitals, were not factors in determining whom they or other bisexual people found attractive. For example, one participant responded, "It is more an attraction to that persons [sic] personality than what is between their legs" (male, bisexual). This indicates a potential difference among participants in defining bisexuality, where some participants indicated that bisexuality meant attraction to more than one gender/sex, whereas others wrote that gender/sex is irrelevant.

Participants were mixed as to whether they described gender as binary. In defining bisexuality, 47 (57.7%) mentions of gender were binary, such as, "[b]isexuality is when an individual is attracted both sexually and romantically to men AND women" (male, bisexual) and, "[a]ttraction in either or both of romantic/sexual, to people who are of the same or opposite sex" (genderqueer, pansexual). Twenty-seven (33.8%) mentions of gender were nonbinary, including descriptions such as, "Having the inclination to feel attracted sexually and/or romantically to people of more than one gender" (female, bisexual), and "as being attracted to people romantically and sexually regardless of their expressed gender" (female, bisexual). These findings indicate that among our participants, a slight majority supports a general definition of bisexuality that uses a binary understanding of gender, though a significant portion of participants explicitly use nonbinary definitions.

In explaining what bisexuality meant to them personally, 32 (59.3%) of responses used a binary construction of gender, as did 36 (54.4%) responses to the question of how they would describe their bisexual identity to someone else. These findings indicate that the slight majority of the participants in our sample discussed bisexuality as attraction to two genders/sexes, and explain their identity to others similarly. Further, 17 (73.9%) responses to the question about what behavior a person needs to exhibit to be bisexual used binary language for gender, as did 25 (64.1%) responses to the questions about what desire a person needs to exhibit to be bisexual.

Some participants stated that whether they described their bisexual identity to others in binary or nonbinary terms depended upon how intelligible they thought nonbinary gender would be to the person to whom they were speaking. For instance, one participant stated:

> Unless I absolutely knew that the other person understood trans* issues and basic queer theory I would just say that I don't care if you are a man or a woman. Leave out the whole in between stuff because sometimes that's a whole other can of worms. (Genderqueer, bisexual)

There were no differences between how pansexual and bisexual people discussed sex or gender across all five questions. Participants were more likely to describe attraction to individuals rather than to gender(s) when describing their bisexual identity to someone else (Question 3) compared to defining bisexuality in general (Question 1) ($\chi^2 = 6.17, p = .013, r = .32$). This indicates that some participants may feel attraction to specific individuals is more salient to their own sexual identity as opposed to bisexuality in general, or it may be that it is easier to explain their identity to others in those terms.

Fluidity

We coded instances of fluidity across all five questions, though primarily in Questions 1 through 3 (defining bisexuality in general, what being bisexual meant to participants personally, and describing their identity to someone else). Within our analysis, the fluidity code included participants' description of bisexuality as encapsulating change in attraction over time. For instance, once participant (male, bisexual) stated, "I'm attracted to those I find attractive, whoever or whatever they may be. I tend to have stronger attraction to men, but it fluctuates sometimes." In this context, fluidity reflects an understanding of bisexuality or sexual attraction as something that is not static and can change within individuals. Discussion of bisexuality as a spectrum or a scale was also coded as fluidity, such as one respondent (female, pansexual) who wrote, "It means being a 2.5ish on the Kinsey scale." Participants' use of fluidity in these instances denotes an understanding of sexuality as a spectrum with many possibilities, as opposed to discrete categories. Finally, participants also discussed how attraction may vary across genders. One participant (male, bisexual) stated, "The types of attraction do not have to be identical for both genders, and the level of attraction does not have to be equal either." In this case, participants' definitions of bisexuality recognize that people may not experience equal attraction to each gender but rather may experience attraction primarily to one gender, or may experience sexual attraction to only one gender and romantic attraction to another.

We also looked at the gender identity of participants who incorporated fluidity into their responses. For Question 1, out of the 11 people who were coded as using fluidity language, six identified as female (18.8% of female participants) and five as male (25% of male participants). For Question 2, six people used fluidity language; two were female (6.3% of female participants) and four were male (20% of male participants). For Question 3, 12 people used fluidity language, including one person who did not disclose their gender identity, two genderqueer people (28.6% of genderqueer participants), seven female people (21.9% of female participants), and two male people (10% of male participants).

Secondary codes

Across the five questions, there were codes that did not fit within the larger themes discussed above. Primary among these were participants' discussion of self-identity and stigma. Notably, there were more codes included in this category for Question 2 compared to Questions 1 and 3, as participants had more unique responses in what being bisexual meant to them personally in contrast to their general definitions of bisexuality or explanation of bisexuality to others. For example, some participants discussed openness as a part of their being bisexual, such as one participant (female, bisexual) who said, "Being bisexual has actually made me a lot more open in my relationships. Because I feel comfortable in my sexuality I encourage my partners to feel the same." Others described their being bisexual as freedom, such as one participant (male, bisexual) who wrote:

> To me, being bisexual is the ultimate, sexual freedom. If I am inclined to date men or women (both cis and trans) or genderqueer people – I can. And, in doing so, I don't need to restructure my personal, sexual identity in order to do it. By being bisexual, I can love whomever I want to love.

For some it was important to not be defined by their sexual identity. One participant (genderqueer, pansexual) wrote, "Being bisexual means that I like both sexes. It doesn't define me and I don't always feel the need to state my sexuality unless it's to relate to someone else and make them feel comfortable about themselves."

Another code within this category for Questions 2 (what being bisexual meant to participants personally) and 3 (describing bisexuality to others) relates to responses indicating stigma. Some described bisexuality in ways that addressed and opposed stereotypes about bisexuality. For instance, one participant (female, bisexual) stated, "I am capable of being attracted to both men and women. That doesn't mean I want to have sex with everyone I meet." These responses indicate that some participants grappled with stereotypes and potentially experiences of stigma related to their bisexuality.

Qualities necessary for bisexual identity

Questions 4 and 5 asked participants to report what behaviors or desires, if any, were necessary for someone to be considered bisexual. For Question 4, none of the participants endorsed the idea that any behavior is necessary for someone to be considered bisexual, and 44 (73.3%) participants expressly stated that no behavior was necessary. This finding demonstrates that behavioral experience is not considered a necessary element to identify as bisexual among the participants. Fifteen (25%) participants did indicate some form of attraction was necessary, indicating a minority of participants endorsed the experience of attraction as a necessary element of bisexuality. The chi-square test comparing bisexual and pansexual participants' responses was significant ($\chi^2 = 4.49$, $p = .034$, $r = .27$), with more bisexual participants than expected (30.61%), and none of the pansexual participants (0%) reporting attraction as necessary to defining oneself as bisexual.

Considering Question 5, 14 (23.3%) of respondents stated that some type of desire was necessary to be considered bisexual, and only eight (13.3%) of respondents explicitly stated that no desire was necessary. Comparing across Questions 4 and 5, more participants were explicit in stating no behavior was necessary compared to the number who stated no desire was necessary, $\chi^2 = 43.98$, $p < .01$, $r = .86$. As such, among our participants, behavior is recognized explicitly by a greater number of participants as an unnecessary requirement of bisexuality compared to the experience of desire.

Discussion

The findings described above shed light on how the young bisexual and pansexual people included in the current study (all of whom stated they felt the label of bisexual applied to them) define and experience bisexuality. Given the low number of statistically significant differences in responses between bisexual and pansexual participants, it appears that both bisexual and pansexual participants define bisexuality in similar ways. The similarity in responses across pansexual and bisexual participants may also be a result of all the participants identifying under the bisexual umbrella. nonmonosexual people, including pansexual people, who explicitly do not identify in this way may view bisexuality differently than do the pansexual people in our sample.

Although much of past research has found people who identify as pansexual are typically younger, in our age-restricted sample, the pansexual participants were older on average than the bisexual participnts. The older age of the pansexual participants may be a result of different identity labels and definitions being socially available to them, or a different sense of agency in choosing sexual identity labels among other possibilities. However, the way gender was discussed suggests that many bisexual participants were aware of the pansexual label, and did not adhere to a binary view of gender. The limitations of this study include the fewer number of pansexual-identified participants in relation to bisexual-identified participants.

Furthermore, the number of participants who identified as another plurisexual identity was too small to be included in our analyses. The experiences and definitions of bisexuality may not reflect the bisexual community broadly as our sample was composed of predominantly White young people.

Defining bisexuality by behavior, attraction, and self-identity

The findings of this study may problematize the use of attraction as a study recruitment criterion for some participants. The majority of participants did not state attraction as a necessary "behavior" or desire" in defining oneself as bisexual, but most did describe various forms of attraction when asked to define bisexuality. The criterion of attraction may make it particularly difficult to recruit pansexual participants, given that none of the pansexual participants in this study reported attraction as a necessary element of bisexual identity. Further, it is apparent in the qualitative data that attraction can mean a number of different things, including sexual, romantic, emotional, or physical, and many participants described bisexuality as including any one of these elements of attraction.

Although health researchers often use behavioral definitions of bisexuality, this does not correspond to the view of bisexuality endorsed by the participants in this study, the majority of whom did not see behavior as a necessary element of bisexuality. This is consistent with previous research that encourages researchers to not assume that measures of self-identity and behavior or attraction are interchangeable (Bauer & Brennan, 2013; Bauer & Jairam, 2008). From a public health standpoint, it is often necessary to examine behavioral variables in relation to sexual health, but self-identity should be prioritized as well to ensure more accurate sampling of the bisexual community. Furthermore, many participants described bisexuality as fluid, which supports the creation and use of measures that assess multiple aspects of sexual orientation. Consistent with this finding, Galupo, Davis, Grynkiewicz, and Mitchell (2014) have noted that measures using dichotomous measures of sex, gender, and sexual orientation may be particularly problematic for bisexual people.

The description of gender in defining bisexuality

There were no differences in how pansexual and bisexual people in the current study discussed sex or gender across all five questions. Although this could be due to the smaller sample size of pansexual people included in this study, these findings do not support the stereotype that bisexual people endorse a binary view of gender while pansexual people do not. Our sample included a substantial proportion of young bisexual people who conceptualize sex or gender as nonbinary, which is in line with how many bisexual advocacy groups, such as the American Institute of Bisexuality and the Bisexual Resource Center, define bisexuality. Further, participants were more likely to mention attraction to specific genders when asked how they would describe their bisexuality to someone else than when describing what being bisexual meant to them personally. This suggests that though participants may perceive gender as being important to others, it may be less salient in relation to their own understanding or experience of bisexuality. This is consistent with the manner in which self-identification was reported throughout the five questions; participant responses were more varied when asked what bisexuality meant to them personally than when asked to define bisexuality in general. The discord between how bisexual people understand their own identity and how that identity is understood by others may be a factor in the higher levels of identity confusion and lower levels of self-disclosure and community connection that Balsam and Mohr (2007) found for their bisexual participants relative to their lesbian/gay peers.

Fluidity

As fluidity came up in participants' responses, largely through Questions 1 through 3, and previous research has indicated that women in general experience more fluidity in their sexual identity than do men (Diamond, 2008), we looked at the frequencies of fluidity endorsement across genders. The findings in this study indicate that there are no consistent differences in the proportion of male and female participants in relation to endorsing fluidity. Larger proportions of male participants included 'fluidity' in their general definition of bisexuality and in describing what bisexual meant to them personally, but a larger proportion of women included fluidity in how they describe their bisexual identity to others. Further research should be conducted to understand whether higher levels of fluidity are found among bisexual men and women in contrast to men and women in the general population. This question may be becoming more relevant, as recent population research indicates that more men are self-identifying as bisexual than ever before (Copen, Chandra, & Febo-Vazquez, 2016).

Potential influence of stigma in defining bisexuality

Another theme identified in the qualitative data was that of stigma related to bisexuality. Some participants stated that they would not bother to define 'pansexuality,' would sometimes conceal their bisexuality to avoid prejudice or invasive questions, or used language that implied they were the target of biphobia when they did disclose their sexuality. This finding is in line with previous research that has indicated pansexual people may face exhaustion from having to explain their identity to others, and thus may avoid doing so (Flanders, Dobinson, & Logie, 2015), as well as research that indicates the disclosure imperative—how discourses on coming out position disclosing one's sexual identity as a "good" part of development while nondisclosure is "bad"—may not apply to bisexual people (McLean, 2007).

The complexity of the "bisexual umbrella"

The intricacies in participants' definitions of bisexuality highlights the extent to which sexual identities are social inventions and/or political constructions (Fonseca & Quintero, 2009; Mitchell et al., 2014). Researchers need to consider the influence of context in defining bisexuality, as identity comes from social practice (Butler, 2010). Sources of external validation and/or repression make it possible to see and recognize particular identities (Jones & Hillier, 2014; Mitchell et al., 2014). Such identities are therefore social, subject to change and negotiation, fluid across time and place, and intersect with other constructions such as age, class, gender, and racialization.

To understand the diversity of sexual minority experience, we need to challenge the assumptions we have about sexuality. As outsiders to heteronormativity and mononormativity (i.e., the privileging attraction to a single gender or sex), bisexual and pansexual people are advantageously located to provide insight into sexual minority identity and experience (Galupo et al., 2014; Gray & Desmaris, 2014; McAllum, 2014; Rust, 2001). Given the complexity of bisexuality, the process whereby individuals define their own bisexuality may be revealing about sexuality in general.

New scientific discourses have made multiple ways of expressing and living sexuality visibly (Galupo, Mitchell, Grynkiewicz, & Davis, 2014). This has made it easier to see and recognize practices (such as polyamory) and identities (such as genderqueer) delegitimized by the dominant constructions of sexuality and gender. Yet such visibility comes with risks. Butler (2010) notes that the "mobilization of identity categories for the purposes of politicization always remain threatened by the prospect of identity becoming an instrument of the power one opposes" (pp. 14–5). Bisexual and pansexual communities may be wary of how their identities are taken up by researchers, which may be in ways that support dominant systems, or systems that facilitate the erasure of the variability and complexity of the bisexual umbrella.

Conclusion

Overall the current research supports the idea that young bisexual and pansexual people define bisexuality in a multitude of ways, and that these definitions not only differ across individuals but also within individuals over different contexts. However, there were few differences between how bisexual and pansexual identified participants defined bisexuality. The data do not support the stereotype that all bisexual people conceptualize gender as binary, or view their own sexuality as binary. Finally, researchers should be careful in how they define bisexuality for the purposes of sampling, and ensure to contextualize their research based on the definitions they use.

References

Albo, B. (2015, September 30). *What does pansexuality mean?* Retrieved from http://dating.about.com/od/glossarywordspq/g/pansexual.htm

Balsam, K. F., & Mohr, J. J. (2007). Adaptation to sexual orientation stigma: A comparison of bisexual and lesbian/gay adults. *Journal of Counseling Psychology, 54*(3), 306–319. doi:10.1037/0022-0167.54.306

Barker, M. J., Bowes-Catton, H., Iantaffi, A., Cassidy, A., & Brewer, L. (2008). British bisexuality: A snapshot of bisexual representations and identities in the United Kingdom. *Journal of Bisexuality, 8*(1/2), 141–162.

Bauer, G. R., & Brennan, D. J. (2013). The problem with 'behavioral bisexuality': Assessing sexual orientation in survey research. *Journal of Bisexuality, 13*(2), 148–165.

Bauer, G. R., Flanders, C. E., MacLeod, M., & Ross, L. E. (2016). Occurrence of multiple mental health or substance use outcomes among bisexuals: A respondent-driven sampling study. *BMC Public Health, 16*, 497. doi:10/1186/s12889-016-3173-z.

Bauer, G. R., & Jairam, J. A. (2008). Are lesbians really women who have sex with women (WSW)? Methodological concerns in measuring sexual orientation in health research. *Women & Health, 48*(4), 383–408.

Butler, J. (2010). *Gender trouble: Feminism and the subversion of identity*. New York, NY: Routledge.

Callis, A. S. (2014). Bisexual, pansexual, queer: Nonbinary identities and the sexual borderlands. *Sexualities, 17*(1/2), 63–80.

Coleman-Fountain, E. (2014). Lesbian and gay youth and the question of labels. *Sexualities, 17* (7), 802–817.

Copen, C. E., Chandra, A., & Febo-Vazquez, I. (2016). *Sexual behavior, sexual attraction, and sexual orientation among adults aged 18–44 in the United States: Data from the 2011–2013 National Survey of Family Growth* (Report No. 88). Retrieved from http://i2.cdn.turner.com/cnn/2016/images/01/06/nhsr88.pdf

Diamond, L. M. (2008). *Sexual fluidity: understanding women's love and desire*. Cambridge, MA: Harvard University Press.

Flanders, C. E. (2015). Bisexual health: A daily diary analysis of stress and anxiety. *Basic and Applied Social Psychology, 37*(6), 319–335. doi:10.1080/01973533.2015.1079202

Flanders, C. E., Dobinson, C., & Logie, C. (2015). "I'm never really my full self": Young bisexual women's perceptions of their mental health. *Journal of Bisexuality, 15*(4), 454–480.

Flanders, C. E., Dobinson, C., & Logie, C. (2016). Young bisexual women's perspectives on the relationship between bisexual stigma, mental health, and sexual health: A qualitative study. *Critical Public Health*. Advance online copy. doi:10.1080/09581596.2016.1158786.

Fonseca, C. H., & Quintero, M. L. S. (2009). La teoría queer: La de-construcción de las sexualidades periféricas [Queer theory: the deconstruction of peripheral sexualities]. *Sociológica* (México), *24*(69), 43–60.

Galupo, M. P. (2011). Bisexuality: complicating and conceptualizing sexual identity. *Journal of Bisexuality, 11*(4), 545–549.

Galupo, M. P., Davis, K. S., Grynkiewicz, A. L., & Mitchell, R. C. (2014). Conceptualization of sexual orientation identity among sexual minorities: Patterns across sexual and gender identity. *Journal of Bisexuality, 14*, 433–456.

Galupo, M. P., Mitchell, R. C., Grynkiewicz, A. L., & Davis, K. S. (2014). Sexual minority reflections on the Kinsey Scale and the Klein Sexual Orientation Grid: Conceptualization and measurement. *Journal of Bisexuality, 14*(3/4), 404–432.

Gray, A. H., & Desmarais, S. (2014). Not all one and the same: Sexual identity, activism, and collective self-esteem. *Canadian Journal of Human Sexuality, 23*(2), 115–122.

Hsieh, H.-F., & Shannon, S. E. (2005). Three approaches to qualitative content analysis. *Qualitative Health Research, 15*(9), 1277–1288.

Jakubowski, K. (2014, November 12). *Pansexuality 101: It's more than 'just another letter.'* Retrieved from http://everydayfeminism.com/2014/11/pansexuality-101/

Jones, T., & Hillier, L. (2014). The erasure of bisexual students in Australian education policy and practice. *Journal of Bisexuality, 14*(1), 53–74.

McAllum, M. A. (2014). "Bisexuality is just semantics...": Young bisexual women's experiences in New Zealand secondary schools. *Journal of Bisexuality, 14*(1), 75–93.

McAllum, M. A. (2015). *"Telling our stories, making it real." Young bisexual women's experiences in New Zealand secondary schools* (Unpublished doctoral dissertation). University of Auckland.

McLean, K. (2007). Hiding in the closet? Bisexuals, coming out and the disclosure imperative. *Journal of Sociology, 43*(2), 151–166.

Mitchell, R. C., Davis, K. S., & Galupo, M. P. (2014). Comparing perceived experiences of prejudice among self-identified plurisexual individuals. *Psychology & Sexuality, 6*(3), 245–257.

Morgan, E. M. (2011). Contemporary issues in sexual orientation and identity development in emerging adulthood. *Emerging Adulthood, 1*(1), 52–66.

Persson, T. J., & Pfaus, J. G. (2015). Bisexuality and mental health: future research directions. *Journal of Bisexuality, 15*(1), 82–98. doi:10.1080/15299716.2014.994694

Rosenthal, A. M., Sylva, D., Safron, A., & Bailey, J. M. (2011). Sexual arousal patterns of bisexual men revisited. *Biological Psychology, 88*(1), 112–115.

Rust, P. C. (2001). Two many and not enough: The meanings of bisexual identities. *Journal of Bisexuality, 1*(1), 31–68.

Appendix

Table of thematic structure

Question	Main Labels	Code
In general, how would you define bisexuality?	Attraction	TYPE:
		General (unspecified)
		Sexual
		Romantic
		Physical
		Emotional
		AND
		OR (also AND/OR)
		Other
	Gender/Sex	Men and women
		Both sexes
		Both genders
		Same and opposite sex
		More than one gender
		Any sex
		Gender doesn't matter
		Gender does matter
		Men, women, nonbinary
		Individuals over gender
		Not need be equal between genders
		Other
	Fluidity	Fluid
		Spectrum
		Not need be equal between genders
	Secondary codes	Capacity or ability for attraction
		Self-identification
		Behavior unnecessary
		Behavior Necessary
		Other
What does being bisexual mean to you personally?	Attraction	TYPE
		General (unspecified)
		Sexual
		Romantic
		Physical
		Emotional
		AND
		OR (also AND/OR)
		Other
	Gender/Sex	Men and women
		Both sexes
		Both genders
		Same and opposite sex
		More than one gender
		Any sex
		Gender doesn't matter
		Gender does matter
		Men, women, nonbinary
		Individuals over gender
		Other
	Fluidity	Fluid
		Spectrum/Scale
		Not need be equal between genders
	Secondary codes	Capacity or ability for attraction
		Self-identification/part of self

(*continued*)

Question	Main Labels	Code
		Behavior unnecessary
		Behavior necessary
		Openness
		More to self than sexuality
		Indication of stigma
		Freedom/Unlimited
		Other
How would you describe your bisexual identity to someone else?	Attraction	TYPE
		General (unspecified)
		Sexual romantic
		Physical emotional
		AND
		OR (also AND/OR)
		Other
	Gender/Sex	Men and women
		Both sexes
		Both genders
		Same and opposite sex
		More than one gender
		Any sex
		Gender doesn't matter
		Gender does matter
		Men, women, nonbinary
		Individuals over gender
		Other
	Fluidity	Fluid
		Spectrum
		Not need be equal between genders
	Secondary codes	Capacity or ability for attraction
		Self-identification
		Behavior unnecessary
		Behavior necessary
		Other
What type of behaviors does a person need to exhibit in order to be bisexual, if any?	Attraction	TYPE
		General (unspecified)
		Sexual
		Romantic
		Physical
		Emotional
		AND
		OR (also AND/OR)
		Other
	Gender/Sex	Men and women
		Both sexes
		Both genders
		Same and opposite sex
		More than one gender
		Any sex
		Gender doesn't matter
		Gender does matter
		Men, women, nonbinary
		Individuals over gender
		Other
	Necessity	Behavior necessary
		Behavior unnecessary
		Attraction necessary
		Attraction unnecessary
		Not need be equal between genders
		Other
	Secondary codes	Self-identification
		Other

(*continued*)

Question	Main Labels	Code
What type of desires does a person need to exhibit in order to be bisexual, if any?	Attraction & Desire	TYPE
		General (unspecified)
		Sexual
		Romantic
		Physical
		Emotional
		AND
		OR (also AND/OR)
		Other
	Gender/Sex	Men and women
		Both sexes
		Both genders
		Same and opposite sex
		More than one gender
		Any sex
		Gender doesn't matter
		Gender does matter
		Men, women, non-binary
		Individuals over gender
		Other
	Necessity	Behavior necessary
		Behavior unnecessary
		Desire necessary
		Desire unnecessary
		Other
	Secondary codes	Self-identification
		Other

What's in a Name? Exploring Pansexuality Online

Christopher K. Belous and Melissa L. Bauman

ABSTRACT
Pansexuality is a growing sexual identity that has become immensely popular in U.S. culture within the previous decade. Currently, little is known about the distinct difference between pansexuality and other sexual orientations/identities; most of what is known comes from popular press and statements by celebrities that have publicly identified as pansexual. As a method of distinguishing and privileging pansexuality as a distinct sexuality, a document and content analysis related to pansexuality was conducted on public blogs and posts from the Internet. Several themes were analyzed, including definition, comparison to bisexuality, identity development, celebrities/media, normalization, and panerasure. Through analysis of 55 unique online posts related to the topic, a proposal consensus statement is offered that attempts to give voice to the pansexual identity as distinctive. In addition, a discussion is offered related to the development and media influence of the pansexual identity—including the emerging concept of panerasure.

Pansexuality is currently not well understood as a distinct identity in U.S. culture—often confused with bisexuality or portrayed negatively in media or popular press. The sexual identity surfaced in the early-to-mid 1990s and has continued to catch our attention with celebrities such as Miley Cyrus, Angel Haze, and Jazz Jennings identifying as such, which has had the added bonus of spreading awareness (Staugenberg, 2015). Since 2004, it has been searched for at ever-increasing rates on Google, with the highest points having occurred since 2012 (Google, 2016). Very few research studies have been conducted attempting to define pansexuality; however, we know the word 'pansexual' is derived from the Greek prefix 'pan' meaning 'all' and reflects individuals who feel they are sexually, emotionally, and spiritually capable of being attracted to any person regardless of gender or sex (Palermo, 2013). Any single study cannot hope to define 'pansexuality,' nor can any definition be all encompassing of people's unique ideas of what pansexuality means to them and its place in their life. Instead, our qualitative document analysis aims to explore the ideas and concepts generated in popular digital media posts widely available on the Internet. Our goal was to understand a representation of how pansexuality is currently being discussed in such a widely accepted and available format.

Sexuality as a construct

Sexual orientation is a multidimensional construct and was not well studied before the work of Kinsey in the late 1940s. He and his colleagues (Kinsey, Pomeroy, & Martin, 1948) developed a scale measuring position on a sexual continuum judging degrees of heterosexuality and homosexuality, thus allowing respondents to be rated on degrees of attraction or activity instead of an 'either/or' dichotomy (Klein, 2014; Ott, Corliss, Wypij, Rosario, & Austin, 2011). Following this work, research regarding sexual identity labels soared as a sociological construct in the 1950s (Scherrer, 2013). Klein (2014) argued that 50 years ago the definition of 'sexual orientation' was simple, as you were either heterosexual or homosexual. However, the Kinsey Scale revealed that there were other possible orientations. Some scholars, including Sigmund Freud, posited that humans are born bisexual, capable of attraction to either males or females before socially constructing a self-identified sexual orientation label (Scherrer, 2013). These initial attempts to define and discuss sexuality focused primarily on the behaviors of the individual, not taking into account beliefs, thoughts, or emotional expressions. Research completed within the previous 30 years has instead focused on larger perspectives of sexual expression to encompass these ideas, and to help realize that sexuality should be seen as an interconnected set of behaviors, feelings, cognitions, actions, beliefs, and values related to how people choose to devote their own personal energy for romantic, physical, spiritual, or other expressions of self and sexuality. This perspective is influenced—in large part—by the gay rights movement, feminism, and the development of queer theory (Marinucci, 2010).

For some, sexual identity labels may provide a sense of community with others who identify in the same manner. Labels offer individuals an opportunity to express themselves and represent their personal journey. The same label provides society with the vocabulary necessary to serve as an important component in conversations regarding privilege and power. However, labels have the power to prescribe our actions and may evoke discrimination (Ferguson, 2015). Klein (2014) stressed that confusion over labels is widespread as his research showed that each individual often poses a different definition of sexual labels.

Definitional concerns and labels

Bisexuality (when not used as an umbrella term) is generally understood as meaning attracted to more than one gender, typically, males or females. Bisexual individuals are the demographic majority among U.S. sexual minorities; some estimates state that approximately 1.8% of the total U.S. population identify as bisexual (Gates, 2011). In addition, bisexuality is the most popular identity of sexual orientation minorities, accounting for 40% of those people who identify as nonheterosexual (Pew Research Center, 2013). The identity of 'bisexual' may include subgroups with individuals who prefer to identify as queer, omnisexual, or pansexual—as these terms are often lumped together as nonheterosexual, nonhomosexual—similar to an "other" category (Barker, 2014; Scherrer, 2013). Few studies have focused on nonbinary individuals aside from bisexuality or fail to differentiate between bisexuality and other plurisexual identities (see Callis, 2014; Galupo, Mitchell, & Davis, 2015). Failure to sufficiently operationalize the term and overlap in popular definitions may be to blame for the scarcity of research.

The definition of bisexuality (when not used as an umbrella term) can be understood as an attraction to both genders—men and women (Barker, 2014). However, 'pansexuality' refers to an extensive range of sexual attractions and expressions making a harmonious definition almost impossible (King, 2011). Plurisexual (attraction to multiple genders or sexes) labels including pansexual, queer, and fluid are not as universally defined as are monosexual or bisexual identities (Galupo et al., 2015). Because American culture depends on binary opposites (male-female, gay-straight) in meaning making, pansexuality represents a gray area not well understood. However, binary definitions limit possibilities for acknowledgement and validation of sexual identity and experiences (Fallas, 2011).

Although Fontanella, Maretti, & Sarra (2014) define 'pansexual' as being attracted to all genders, others define the term as an identity that denounces gender or sex as a defining feature of sexuality, despite the "heteronormative understanding of human sexuality which views people as dichotomously attracted to 'same gender' or 'opposite gender'" (Barker, 2014, p. 170; Gonel, 2013). Because there is no uniform definition of 'pansexuality,' it is often confused or combined with omnisexual, plurisexual, polysexual, or queer– orientations that also suffer from deficient definitions. One study found that 60% of participants who reported being attracted to "both genders" endorsed more than one sexual identity (Galupo et al., 2015). Those who identify as pansexual may choose another identity label (e.g., gay, lesbian) more widely known by society to avoid having to explain pansexuality in social situations (Gonel, 2013).

Individuals have the power to attribute meaning to and comprehension of their sexual identities regardless of the existence of socially constructed labels (Horowitz & Newcomb, 2002). Scholars speculate pansexuality is gaining acceptance and membership—especially among millennials and 'generation Z'—due to the broad and flexible definition allowing for the freedom of choice and self-identification regarding sexual expression (Callis, 2014; Gonel, 2013; Staugenberg, 2015). Others argue that the term is so broad it contradicts the purpose of a label, similar to the postulate of queer theory (Marinucci, 2010; Palermo, 2013). Gonel (2013) believes individuals who identify as pansexual actually embody the stance of antilabeling or choose a label (pansexuality) that encompasses a wide variety of expressions limiting the need to fit into a single category or identity. Pansexuality is quickly becoming the face of the antilabeling movement within a new generation. There is a clear connection between pansexuality as an antilabel and the continued reclamation of the word 'queer' throughout the gay rights movement, and developed more fully within queer theory (Halperin, 1997).

Media

Popular media often portrays negative views and stereotypes of sexual minorities (Belous, Wampler, & Warmels-Herring, 2015). Sexual identities deviating from the binary have often been represented in literature and media as confused, a transitional stage between heterosexuality and homosexuality, or denial of one's 'true' sexual orientation (Horowitz & Newcomb, 2002). Lack of acceptance for nonheterosexual identities may foster fear in individuals who identify as such, or cause them to embody the characteristics of the few socially accepted role models visible in the media (Belous et al., 2015). Unfortunately, the list of visible pansexual role models is severely limited. GLAAD's 2013 to 2014 "Where we are on TV" report counted 46[1] LGBTQ+ characters on popular shows, but only 10 were bisexual and none identified with another plurisexual label. Previous research has shown the significant influence of the media on the development of sexual identity (e.g., Slater, 2007), and specifically for nonheterosexual populations (e.g., Belous et al., 2015; Gomillion & Giuliano, 2011). Media representation has played an important part in the advancement of equality for LGBTQ+ individuals and also provides an opportunity for increased public awareness, identity affirmation, positive role modeling, normalization, and destruction of negative stereotypes (Cunningham, 2015). Specifically, pansexuality has gained popularity in the media after Miley Cyrus declared herself pansexual. In fact Google reported the word was among the top search terms in the months following the announcement (Grinberg, 2015). Other celebrities have followed suit making their pansexuality known and contributing to the increase in pan-awareness. Increasing acceptance for the identity led to the recent creation of Pansexual Pride Day celebrated on December 8.

Importance of study

For decades in a society where only three major sexual identities (heterosexual, homosexual, bisexual) are recognized, people have been trying to fit themselves into these categories that may not accurately describe their identity or experiences (Drobac, 1999; Horowitz & Newcomb, 2002). Erasure of bisexuality or bisexual invisibility is a common occurrence in which the legitimacy of bisexuality is questioned, and in the most extreme circumstances, denied (GLAAD, 2015; Yoshino, 2000). If a woman identifies as bisexual but is dating a woman she is presumed a lesbian. Should the same woman date a man, she would incur the label of 'heterosexual.' Bisexuality and other sexual minority labels are often misunderstood and marginalized by heterosexual and homosexual populations (Fallas, 2011; Scherrer, 2013). The same is becoming true for the pansexual identity label. Despite its growing presence and awareness in the media, erasure of pansexuality is becoming a regular phenomenon with potentially devastating effects. One study found that more than one half of individuals identifying as pansexual were not involved with any LGBTQ+ organizations due to the fact that pansexuality was not adequately represented to meet their needs, or discrimination from LGBTQ+ individuals (Gonel, 2013). Through the research and creating an awareness of the legitimacy of the pansexual identity, hopefully the impact of panerasure will be decreased.

Method

This qualitative study examined the published expression of a pansexual identity, definition, or description, within the public domain of posted material on the Internet. Document analysis has long been accepted as a method through which to create meaning related to the presentation of social ideology and perception (Bowen, 2009; Prior, 2003). In addition, document analysis—particularly as it relates to the hermeneutic process of interpretation—has been described as ideal for use in research with marginalized populations (Altheide, 2000).

The authors are well versed in sexual minority literature and research methods. In addition to having completed several studies previously in the field of LGBTQ+ studies, both have significant experience in working with sensitive populations in various settings including social service agencies and psychotherapy. They approach the research with a bias toward positive expression of sexuality and identity.

Data selection

The authors conducted an Internet search with the most popular search engines (Google.com, Bing.com, Yahoo.com) to gather posts from media outlets, personal websites, educational forums, blogs, news reports, and so on, that attempted to explain or define the term 'pansexual.' We did not limit the search to a specific geographic location, so the blogs and websites could have been designed, written, or hosted in countries from anywhere in the world. However, all pages and data points were in English, and a vast majority had the ".com" URL extension (as opposed to other, country specific extensions such as ".co.uk"). Assumptions can be made that most results were based in the United States. Search terms included (both combined together and used as separate search terms): *pan, pansexual, pan sexual, pan-sexual, identity, definition*. In addition, nonsingular search terms were used by searching for statements about pansexuality. These included What is a pansexual? What does it mean to be pansexual? What is the definition of *pansexual*? Who is pansexual? What is a pansexual identity?

As we wanted the largest representative sample we could find, we went through the first 50 pages of the results with each search term—selecting each link and determining whether the post was appropriate for use. Suitability was determined through the evaluation of three criteria (answers to the question being "yes"): (1) Does the post/website posit a definition of pansexuality? (2)

Is the post directly related to the identity of pansexuality? (3) Does the post describe the differences between pansexuality and other identities—or the uniqueness of the identity? This process resulted in a total sample of $N = 55$ posts for analysis. Of the 55, 10 (18%) were from personal blogs (e.g., Tumblr, WordPress), 14 (25%) were posts from their own domain, 8 (15%) were from news outlets (e.g., CNN), 20 (36%) were from magazine articles/websites (e.g., *Huffington Post*), and only 3 (5%) were from universities or educational centers (e.g., Columbia University). For a complete breakdown and citation of each source used, please refer to supplemental materials.

Analytic procedures

Data analysis included a three stage process of examination: (1) skimming, (2) reading, (3) interpretation (Bowen, 2009). All 55 posts that were gathered and deemed suitable for examination went through this process. Due to the repetitious nature of postings on the Internet, and the proliferation of cross-postings related to this topic specifically, the sample gathered can be seen as a good representation of the topic in online forums.

Skimming included the brief consideration of each article, determining suitability. This process was completed during data selection as a first pass—to be confirmed by the alternate author when a single author discovered a datum. Reading occurred separately, whereby each author read the post for general understanding and to begin the process of getting comfortable with the data; identifying intuitive in-vivo thematic elements of meaning evident in the data. In Stage 3, interpretation, the authors separately went through each document and called attention to text and images that fit into the following categories: definition, comparison to bisexuality, identity development, celebrity, normalization, and panerasure. These categories were preselected to elicit the specific results necessary to answer the main research question, a common method within thematic analysis (Fereday & Muir-Cochrane, 2006). Both authors independently engaged in all stages; however, in Stage 3, the pair completed final thematic analysis in conjunction.

In the examination of the theme 'definition,' the authors physically combined the different definitions through a hermeneutic method to interpret the data (Paterson & Higgs, 2005). To determine the most pronounced definitional characteristics, we separated out the text from each coding scheme and input them into a text analyzer (Textalyser.net) that counted words and phrases to gather information on the most-used statements. This allowed us to see the influence of word usage and determine the most effective words to use in interpretation.

Results

As of the writing of this article, there were 379,000+ results on Google when the search term 'pansexual' was entered. On Bing, 995,000+ results are available, and on Yahoo!, 935,000+ webpages are listed. The lower number available on Google was due to the algorithms used to determine viable/unique websites—Bing and Yahoo! include websites regardless of whether they are repetitious in the results. In following the methods and procedures outlined above for data collection and analysis, we were able to support our thematic elements and coalesce the information into meaningful statements.

Comparison between bisexual and pansexual identities

Virtually all of the data points we were able to identify had an element of comparing bisexual and pansexual identities. Most identified pansexuality as a subset or component of a bisexual identity, "Pansexual people are bisexual, in-fact; however, bisexuality does not place the same emphasis on sexual and gender identity awareness, but more simply indicates attraction to the two (generally accepted) biological sexes" (Stop Homophobia). Some discuss the difference between the two as focused on gender, such as this statement: "It's different from bisexuality. Bisexuality refers to people attracted to men and women. With more people identifying across the gender spectrum between men and women, pansexuality has emerged as a catch-all that includes everyone else" (Difference Between). However, as is noticeable in the previous statements, there is still a high degree of overlap between bisexuality and pansexuality—something that is often reflected in online statements such as: "The distinction between 'pansexual' and 'bisexual' is still up for debate, with no consensus on the best terminology" (Grinberg, 2015)

To try to create a better sense of the difference between the terms, some authors attempted to use the person's gender identity as a qualifying characteristic. For example,

> ... not generalizing their dating patterns on same sex or opposite sex candidates only. A lot of pan-gender people do not represent themselves as a male or female also, there is a sense of free thinking with them, and they enjoy being able to express themselves as a human with interests in other humans; not necessarily stating they are men or women. (No Bullying.com)

The argument could be made that this may be one of the distinct differences between bisexual and pansexual identities: gender expression of the individual whose identity is being negotiated. However, there is no data with regard to the relative numbers of people who identify as pansexual and those who identify as gender-queer, queer, or gender nonspecific (etc.).

Panerasure

Much of the debate around pansexuality stems from the push-back from other members of the LGBTQ+ community related to the pluralization of sexual attraction orientations.

> There is a feeling that pansexual people are simply avoiding the bisexual label due to the stigmas associated with it (that bisexual people are simply greedy and promiscuous, and

> spread disease among both the heterosexual and homosexual communities). Conversely, many in the pansexual community feel as though these beliefs are forms of prejudice and pansexual erasure. (Difference Between)

This is just one element that is leading to the stigmatization and minimization of pansexuality as a unique and distinct sexual orientation. Some bloggers and online personalities who identify as pansexual have posted personal stories of trying to come out and the struggles associated with talking with their friends about what pansexuality is.

> I am a queer woman. I flip-flop between identities. I have been "straight," then "bisexual," then "pansexual," ... I often feel "not gay enough" to hang out in queer spaces; I feel like an intruder or a wannabe. I have had friends "jokingly" tell me that I should "just pick a side already." And sometimes I actually contemplate it; I would just be happier being straight, and I wouldn't have to deal with homophobia as frequently! Besides some men are hot. I could deal with being straight. Then I see a pretty girl, so I think, "I'll just be a lesbian." ... See the problem? (Charbonneau)

This is just one of many examples of what happens when the ambiguity related to the lack of acceptance of identity has led to confusion of self and social position. Most of the posts mention something of the sort related to the statement, "I am discriminated against, with people telling me that I just haven't made up my mind" (Shiner).

Definition

Determining a cohesive definition based on the lived experiences of 'real life'—aka, the posts of the average person on the Internet—was a rather straightforward process. After the identification of text segments that identified a specific definition for pansexuality, we input all the text into a word-count and frequency analyzer. There were 1,638 total words used in all the samples, and 489 unique words. The word 'gender' was the most frequently used (3.8%) individual word in the definitions, with a prominence rating of 48.1; followed by 'people' at 43.3 (1.9%). Two-word phrases had 'attracted to' as the most popular (1.7%, prominence > 47.9); "regardless of" coming in second (.5%, prominence > 55.9). When the scope was widened to three-word sections, the highest prominence was in the phrase (or directly related) 'all gender identities' (prominence > 70%). This process was performed to determine the most frequently and widely used phrases to determine an appropriate definitional supposition that would encompass the largest range of current ideas.

In doing the analysis, it became apparent quickly that there were some very repetitious definitions and phrases used when discussing pansexuality. This could be mainly due to the fact that in posting content to personal blogs, educational outlets, and so on, there is a tendency to directly copy over and reuse materials from other similar websites. For this section, many posts repeated the vernacular breakdown of the word 'pansexual,' describing it as, "Coming from the Greek prefix 'pan,' meaning 'all' … and sexual" (e.g., Evans). However, authors would then describe how even though the word's development breaks down to 'all sexual' it does not mean that a pansexual person will have promiscuous or open sex with anyone. They state, "pansexuality does not mean being attracted to everyone… many pansexual people have biological or physical preferences" (e.g., Stop Homophobia). However, all posts agreed that pansexual people are "open to attraction regardless of gender identity" (e.g., Go Ask Alice). This distinction of being what some consider 'gender blind' allows the identity holder to develop relationships with people instead of gender identities. It is important to note that in almost all attempts made to define pansexuality that we found, there was most often a qualification added to the definition specifying that a pansexual person, "does [or 'will'] not want to have sex with everyone…" (e.g., Entertainment Daily). This is an important distinction as there are many people who could use the linguistic origins of the word to mean that a pansexual person is interested in having sex with anyone and everyone.

Identity development

The development of a pansexual identity was described as having specific requirements. "Recognition of the existence of different genders and sexualities is a major aspect of pansexuality identity" (Shangraw). Such statements indicate that it is not simply enough to say that you are a pansexual person; that the identity of being pansexuality requires fundamental beliefs to be embraced. Some authors describe the process of discovering their true identity as a natural element of the growing acceptance of diversity within generational differences:

> young people are using more nuanced ways of describing themselves, pulling in factors like spirituality and intellect in addition to physical attraction… young people know exactly what they want and who they are, and they're crafting language to represent that. (Glum)

Some people have begun to embrace pansexual identities as a component of their relationship to their significant other, particularly as it relates to relationships where a member of a relationship may transitions into a different gender identity, or confirms a gender non-specific identity. For example, "sexual identity [may change] according to the gender to which their partner has transitioned, an increasing number have chosen to self-label as pansexual, queer, or one of the other non-monosexual identities" (Stop Homophobia).

Celebrities and media

It is undeniable how influential media and celebrities are to the social climate of any culture. In terms of the pansexual identity, in recent years there has been a widespread influx of popular figures who have come out and spoken about pansexual ideas. These include superstars such as Miley Cyrus, who identifies as pansexual, stating,

> I am literally open to every single thing that is consenting and doesn't involve an animal and everyone is of age. Everything that's legal, I'm down with. Yo, I'm down with any adult–anyone over the age of 18 who is down to love me. I don't relate to being boy or girl, and I don't have to have my partner relate to boy or girl. (Petrusich, 2015)

This coincides with the definitions stated by others. Other influential celebrities such as Kristen Stewart, Andrew Garfield, Ruby Rose, Josh Hutcherson, and Shailene Woodley have spoken out about pansexual acceptance, either from identifying as such, or professing a need for increased visibility of the identity in media. Individuals identifying as pansexual are even out in elected positions, such as Mary Gonzalez, a Texas state representative, who publicly stated she was pansexual in 2012.

Normalization

In much of the data we collected, statements were included that normalized pansexuality as a typical part of our evolving culture. "The new enlightened identity among famous millennials is to be 'pansexual,' 'omnisexual,' or 'sexually fluid.' … it's not quite the same as being bisexual… it is spawned by a cultural shift towards tolerance and diverse experiences" (Peterkin). Many of the celebrities and personalities that are expressing these views are using their social position to increase awareness and diversify acceptance, such as when Mary Gonzalez stated, "… they really like me and they hear my story. And well, you know, I think that they start to at least change their minds a little bit" (Signorile, 2015). The process of famous household names identifying and discussing this topic leads to higher rates of acceptance and awareness, thereby decreasing stigmatization of sexual expression. When athlete Tom Daley came out in an online video, he did not state a specific sexual orientation identity, merely that he was still attracted to women, but was currently in a same-gender (male-male) relationship. One blogger commented on this, stating, "Daley's choice of words, however deliberate, highlights [the] growing acceptance of the new sexual fluidity" (Brisbane). Even though Daley did not mention that he was specifically pansexual, many people believe that his statements (and those of others) will help "more people self-identify as queer … or pansexual…, [and] society will hopefully become more accepting of those who do not restrict their sexual preferences to a certain gender" (Khoja).

Discussion

In doing this research, it became obvious that there was a plethora of thoughts, feelings, and perceptions of pansexuality across the Internet. However, we were also very quick to realize that those different thoughts all shared several common themes, and the vast majority were very positive toward acceptance and awareness of pansexuality as an identity. The biggest overall outcome of this research is this: bisexuality does not equal pansexuality. They are unique sexual identities and orientations with distinct characteristics.

Pansexuality is a normal and increasingly common option for self-identification. Through the widespread acceptance and visibility of famous persons who are identifying with this label, there is a growing level of exposure and acceptance, and thereby many people are realizing that there are more options when considering how they can self-identify. They are realizing that because they did not fit with the standard, well-known, three sexual identity models (heterosexual, gay/lesbian, or bisexual) there are emerging identities that they can relate to—and that is OK. One of the ways in which this message is being spread is through the ever-increasing prevalence of social media, blog, and news posts that positively discuss a pansexual identity from a normalizing perspective.

Location of pansexuality

Throughout the data and literature examined, pansexuality was consistently considered 'under the umbrella' of bisexuality. This research, and other research, begs the question: Is it possible that bisexuality is a component of pansexuality, as opposed to the expressed idea that pansexuality is under the 'umbrella' of bisexuality? 'Pansexuality' as a term and identity is much larger and more encompassing, though many definitions proposed for bisexuality are much narrower. This may indicate a need for the restructuring of the sexual orientation continuum to include pansexuality as a larger categorical identity under which bisexuality exists—as a specific subset of pansexual orientations. More research is needed in this area to clarify.

Research implications

This article is a purely exploratory study on the discussions and posts of popular content off the internet. More research is needed in several areas, including the location of pansexuality as an identity—and where it belongs in relation to other identities. Ever since the recognition of different sexual identities (mostly due to Alfred Kinsey's sexological research), researchers have been placing and categorizing sexual orientations on continuums and in relation to one another. As pansexuality is one of the newest orientations to be identified and is gaining widespread acceptance, it would be important to make sure that it was considered fully in the context of what it means as it relates to the other identities.

One way to get such information to more fully discover the intricacies of the pansexual identity would be to conduct qualitative and quantitative research related to the personal identity of pansexual persons. Specifically, research is needed on the difference between bisexual identities and pansexual identities to tease out the exact difference between bisexual and pansexuality. In addition, an understanding of the stigma and discrimination/animosity between sexual orientations could be helpful in understanding the development process of being a pansexual person.

Practice implications

The present study may be helpful for clinicians, policy makers, and those working in social service agencies. Many therapists, counselors, psychologists, and social workers who are gay affirmative already utilize a process to empower their clients to self-identify their sexual orientations and do not force clients to pick from a list of options. However, due to the newness of pansexuality, many have not had the chance to update documentation options or to engage in training efforts. With newer and more information being readily available, hopefully clinicians can consider the usage of the information within their clinical practice.

Those in social service agencies can use the information discovered in this article to inform programming opportunities, particularly as it relates to working with minors around sexual orientation and self-discovery. Sex educators who embrace a comprehensive model should include elements of pansexuality in their workshops and programs, as well as the training of educators and administrators. Although pansexuality is developing and becoming more widely accepted, it is far from being a commonly understood identity. As such, incorporating pansexuality into discussions and options can help to promote acceptance. In addition, following in the footsteps of Representative Gonzalez, committing to creating inclusive and accepting policy at all levels of society—especially governmental—can truly help lessen the stigma of pansexuality.

Limitations

This study examined pansexual identity and the discussion of the orientation on popular Internet websites and posts of content. Such information/public posts have often not undergone rigorous review—only having been edited for clarity by type editors and proofreaders. This means much of the data collected was the personal opinion of the author, and not empirical research. However, it should be noted that many of the authors identified themselves as pansexual and so could be considered experts discussing their own sexual identities. In addition, we found many cross-linked and -posted articles and text segments. This repetitious posting of information may influence the overall ideas and stifle the creation of new meaning. In addition, only websites and posts that were optimized for search engines were easily found, and so it is possible that many entries were not able to be found.

Document and content analysis is widely considered a valid method of synthesizing meaning associated with large volumes of already published or created data. However, it is also known to have many limitations, such as having a subjective bias, being situational and influenced by popular opinions at the time of writing, and using documents whose authors did not originally write them to be used for research purposes. We attempted to counter these limitations through the consistent use of an analytical plan; however we admit that these limitations still may have affected our results.

In addition, definitions of sexual identity are intensely personal for each individual. We acknowledge that we are not experts in any one person's life and privilege their own process. This is an academic endeavor to engage in the process of understanding and promoting social change of the pansexual identity. We encourage each person to use this information as a starting point, and not an ending point, on the discussion of this identification.

Note

1. 'LGBTQ+' is a term used to identify individuals who identify on the sexuality spectrum as non-heterosexual. Specifically, the acronym stands for lesbian, gay, bisexual, trans*, queer, and the + stands for all other identities not already stated in an effort to be inclusive.

References

Altheide, D. L. (2000). Tracking discourse and qualitative document analysis. *Poetics, 27*(4), 287–299. New York, NY: Springer. doi:10.1016/S0304-422X(00)00005-X

Barker, M. (2014). Bisexuality. In T. Teo (Ed.), *Encyclopedia of critical psychology* (pp. 170–175). doi:10.1007/978-1-4614-5583-7_28

Belous, C. K., Wampler, R. S., & Warmels-Herring, T. (2015). Gay male adaptation in the coming out process. *Journal of Gay & Lesbian Mental Health, 19*(1), 55–71. doi:10.1080/19359705.2014.921265

Bowen, G. A. (2009). Document analysis as a qualitative research method. *Qualitative Research Journal, 9*(2), 27–40. doi:10.3316/QRJ0902027

Callis, A. S. (2014). Bisexual, pansexual, queer: Non-binary identities and the sexual borderlands. *Sexualities, 17*(1/2), 63–80. doi:10.1177/1363460713511094

Cunningham, A. (2015, June 25). We should hear more about pansexuality on TV [web log post]. Retrieved from http://www.opinionpanel.co.uk/2015/06/25/pansexuality-in-the-media/

Drobac, J. A. (1999). Pansexuality and the law. *William and Mary Journal of Women and the Law, 297*, 1–11.

Fallas, J. A. (2011). *Disrupting patriarchal norms and languages: Narrative and rhetorical analyses of bi and pansexual feminist blogs* (Unpublished doctoral dissertation). Retrieved from ProQuest. (3533447).

Fereday, J., & Muir-Cochrane, E. (2006). Demonstrating rigor using thematic analysis: A hybrid approach of inductive and deductive coding and theme development. *International Journal of Qualitative Methods, 5*(1), 80–92. doi:10.1177/160940690600500107

Ferguson, S. (2015, January 14). Labels: Empowering, harmful, or both? *Everyday Feminism.* Retrieved from http://everydayfeminism.com/2015/01/labels-empowering-harmful/

Fontanella, L., Maretti, M., & Sarra, A. (2014). Gender fluidity across the world: A multilevel item response theory approach. *Quality and Quantity, 48*, 2253–2568. doi:10.1007/s11135-013-9907-4

Galupo, M. P., Mitchell, R. C., & Davis, K. S. (2015). Sexual minority self-identification: Multiple identities and complexity. *Psychology of Sexual Orientation and Gender Diversity, 2*(4), 355–364. http://dx.doi.org/10.1037/sgd0000131

Gates, G. J. (2011). *How many people are lesbian, gay, bisexual, and transgender?* [press release; demographic data]. The Williams Institute. Retrieved from http://williamsinstitute.law.ucla.edu/wp-content/uploads/Gates-How-Many-People-LGBT-Apr-2011.pdf

GLAAD. (2015). *Erasure of bisexuality.* Gay and Lesbian Alliance Against Discrimination. Retrieved from http://www.glaad.org/bisexual/bierasure

Gomillion, S. C., & Giuliano, T. A. (2011). The influence of media role models on gay, lesbian, and bisexual identity. *Journal of Homosexuality, 58*(3), 330–354. doi:10.1080/00918369.2011.546729

Gonel, A. H. (2013). Pansexual identification in online communities: Employing a collaborative queer method to study pansexuality. *Graduate Journal of Social Science, 10*(1), 36–59.

Google. (2016, June 1). *Pansexual.* Google Trends. Retrieved from http://www.google.com/trends.

Grinberg, E. (2015, November 9). What it means to be pansexual. *CNN.* Retrieved from http://www.cnn.com/2015/11/09/living/pansexual-feat/

Halperin, D. (1997). *Saint Foucault: Towards a gay hagiography.* New York, NY: Oxford University Press.

Horowitz, J. L., & Newcomb, M. D. (2002). A multidimensional approach to homosexual identity. *Journal of Homosexuality, 42*(2), 1–19. doi:10.1300/J082v42n02_01

King, A. R. (2011). Environmental influences on the development of female college students who identify as multiracial/biracial-bisexual/pansexual. *Journal of College Student Development, 52*(4), 440–455.

Kinsey, A. C., Pomeroy, W. B., & Martin, C. E. (1948). *Sexual behavior in the human male.* Philadelphia, PA: Saunders.

Klein, F. (2014). Are you sure you're heterosexual? Or homosexual? Or even bisexual? *Journal of Bisexuality, 14*, 341–346. doi:10.1080/15299716.2014.953282

Marinucci, M. (2010). *Feminism is queer: The intimate connection between queer and feminist theory.* New York, NY: Zed.

Ott, M. Q., Corliss, H. L., Wypij, D., Rosario, M., & Austin, S. B. (2011). Stability and change in self-reported sexual orientation identity in young people: Application of mobility metrics. *Archives of Sexual Behavior, 40*, 519–532. doi:10.1007/s10508-010-9691-3

Palermo, E. (2013, November 12). Pansexual: A 'new' sexual orientation? *Live Science.* Retrieved from http://www.livescience.com/41163-pansexual-sexual-orientation-pansexuality.html

Paterson, M., & Higgs, J. (2005). Using hermeneutics as a qualitative research approach in professional practice. *The Qualitative Report, 10*(2), 339–357. Retrieved from http://nsuworks.nova.edu/tqr/vol10/iss2/9

Petrusich, A. (2015, June 9). Free to be Miley. *Paper Mag*. Retrieved from http://www.papermag.com/free-to-be-miley-1427581961.html

Pew Research Center. (2013). *A survey of LGBT Americans* [press release, demographic report]. Pew Research Center. Retrieved from http://www.pewsocialtrends.org/2013/06/13/a-survey-of-lgbt-americans/.

Prior, L. (2003). *Using documents in social research*. Thousand Oaks, CA: Sage.

Scherrer, K. (2013). Culturally competent practice with bisexual individuals. *Clinical Social Work, 41*, 238–248. doi:10.1007/s10615-013-0451-4

Signorile, M. (May 29, 2015). Mary Gonzalez, first openly pansexual legislator explains how she is changing minds in Texas. *Huffpost Queer Voices*. Retrieved from http://www.huffingtonpost.com/2015/05/29/mary-gonzalez-pansexual_n_7433432.html

Slater, M. D. (2007). Reinforcing spirals: The mutual influence of media selectivity and media effects and their impact on individual behavior and social identity. *Communication Theory, 17*(3), 281–303. doi:10.1111/j.1468-2885.2007.00296.x

Staugenberg, J. (2015, August 31). Pansexual: What is it - and when did the term gain popularity? *Independent*. Retrieved from http://www.independent.co.uk/life-style/love-sex/panseual-miley-cyrus-what-is-it-and-when-did-the-word-become-popular-104769640.html.

Yoshino, K. (2000). The epistemic contract of bisexual erasure. *Stanford Law Review, 52*(2), 353–461.

Perceptions of Individuals Who Are Non-monosexuals held by Graduate Students: A Q Methodological Study

Colton Brown, Diane Montgomery, and Tonya R. Hammer

ABSTRACT

"Non-monosexual" is an umbrella term for bisexual, pansexual, queer, and fluid+ identities, and it lacks visibility and acceptance in the larger LGBTQ+ community. Research has shown that non-monosexual experience more discrimination than their monosexual peers (. Q methodology was used to explore the perceptions that graduate students have of the non-monosexual community, with 19 participants sorting 40 statements addressing stereotypes of non-monosexuals. Using a principal components factor analysis with varimax rotation and a significance level of .50, two factors were interpreted as, "We're all Okay," characterized by social acceptance and normalization of non-monosexuals and "You Might be Okay," implying an individual acceptance of those who are non-monosexual, but lack of assurance on the place of non-monosexuals in society/communities. To further explain factor interpretation, two monologues are presented that represent theoretical findings for non-monosexuals for each factor. The discussion of these findings is framed from a social justice perspective oriented toward increasing acceptance of non-monosexual individuals.

Non-monosexuality refers to sexual orientations that fall along the spectrum of sexuality, as opposed to polar ends of the gay/straight binary (Goodman, 2013). Common non-monosexual identities include, but are not limited to, bisexual, pansexual, and queer. Importantly, the method of defining non-monosexuality differs based on the emphasis one takes in identifying sexual orientations (for more information, see Barker, Richards, & Bowes-Cotton, 2009; Morgan & Thompson, 2007). It is important to understand how others perceive this community, as members often report experiencing discrimination form heterosexuals and their lesbian and gay counterparts (Hoang, Holloway, & Mendoza, 2011). This study specifically sought to understand how graduate students from varying fields perceive this community. We chose the graduate student population because they consistently affect the larger undergraduate population and have a broad sphere of influence (Bettinger, Long, & Taylor, 2016).

Perceptions of non-monosexuals

Much of the literature on non-monosexuality focuses on bisexual individuals, as they are the most commonly referenced group under this umbrella. From this literature, various stereotypical ideas of bisexual people arise, including assumptions that they are all nonmonogamous and polyamorous (Israel & Mohr, 2004), that they are in a transitionary phase between heterosexual and gay/lesbian (Meyer, 2003), and that they are confused by their attractions to multiple sexes or genders (Fox, 1991). Although some non-monosexual individuals may exhibit some of these qualities, these stereotypical ideas are often used to disenfranchise the non-monosexual community. Additionally, members of this community face degrading self-perceptions, such as low self-worth and anxiety in social relationships due to negative experiences in their communities and in prior relationships. These negative experiences include biphobia (Jorm, Korten, Rodgers, Jacomb, & Christensen, 2002), discrimination (Hoang et al., 2011), and isolation (Dentato, 2011).

Experiences of sexual minorities on college campuses

College is a common time for lesbian, gay, bisexual, transgender, and queer (LGBTQ) individuals to develop better understandings of their sexualities (Beemyn & Rankin, 2011). The university environment may have significant impacts on LGBTQ individuals' self-perceptions (Pascarella & Terenzini, 2005). Students may choose not to come out if they perceive their university to be a hostile environment (Rankin, Weber, Blumenfeld, & Frazer, 2010). These findings are of significance because discrimination on college campuses is still a common occurrence. The State of Higher Education Survey, with more than 5,000 participants, indicated that LGBTQ students experience discrimination on college campuses ranging from subtle to extreme forms (Rankin et al., 2010). Respondents to this survey included undergraduate students, graduate students, faculty, and administration, with the highest percentage being undergraduates.

Woodford, Kulick, Sinco, and Hong (2014) found covert and overt forms of harassment toward sexual minorities on campuses. They noted that harassment may be difficult to identify because subtle forms, such as microaggressions, seem to be the dominant shape harassment takes (Woodford et al., 2014). Hong, Woodford, Long, and Renn (2016) found similar results studying undergraduate and graduate LGBTQ students, with the most prevalent forms of harassment and stereotyping involving subtle forms of heterosexism. Although these studies reflect that heterosexism and discrimination are present on college campuses, they do not solely focus on perceptions of graduate students.

Prior research has demonstrated that individuals who receive more education are often more open to diversity and differences between themselves and others

(Pew Research Center, 2016). These differences in openness to diversity and education provide a rationale for studying graduate students' perceptions separately from their undergraduate peers. Additionally, these studies do not acknowledge the differing perceptions individuals may have toward subgroups within the LGBTQ community. This study was designed to explore this gap in the literature and highlight how graduate students specifically perceive non-monosexuals.

Research question

Based on our review of the literature, the following research question was developed: What characteristics do graduate students assign to non-monosexuality and non-monosexuals? Negative stereotypes of non-monosexuals largely informed the research question and statements selected from the concourse. A "concourse" refers to available discourse and data on a given topic (Brown, 1980), that is, research, writings, and conversations on non-monosexuality. We chose to focus specifically on graduate students because of their spheres of influence and the role they can play in enhancing others' lives, such as enhancing undergraduates' college experiences through teaching (Bettinger et al., 2016). The perceptions graduate students have of non-monosexual people may contribute to a lack of authentic connection or awareness or may encourage authenticity and acceptance.

Method

We employed Q methodology as the research strategy to describe the perceptions of graduate students toward non-monosexuality and individuals who are non-monosexual. Q methodology was originated by William Stephenson (1953) and seeks to study subjectivity of phenomenon (Watts & Stenner, 2005). Subjectivity captures the feelings and beliefs of participants toward a topic (Stephenson, 1973, 1980), in our case, responses to stereotypes of non-monosexuality. This method was chosen due to the impact social positionality and perspectives have on discussions of sexuality. Q methodology acknowledges that individuals will view a topic differently from others based on their experiences and may respond differently to a topic over time (McKeown & Thomas, 2013). This feature of Q methodology is of specific importance for this study, as society has become more accepting of LGBTQ individuals over time. This study is grounded as an account of participants' perceptions at a specific point in history.

Additionally, Q methodology subscribes to an abductive method of generating theory from data (Watts & Stenner, 2012). Abduction was important in this study because much of the theory and data on non-monosexuals are not exclusive to them; rather, results are often nested in theory and data that address gay and lesbian issues. Using Q methodology allows for distinct analysis of non-monosexuality through the lens of shared viewpoints across participants. In this study, we explore how the feelings and beliefs of graduate students can be measured and clustered together to provide general viewpoints. Results indicate how by-person sorts cluster together to formulate factors that demonstrate similarities among participants. The data are analyzed by entire person viewpoints and not by individual statements, items, or responses.

Participants

We invited 19 graduate students to participate in this study. Participants were gathered through convenience sampling drawn from our established networks of graduate students in various fields of psychology, higher education leadership, and communication. Ages of participants ranged from 23 to 46 years old with seven females and 12 males. Participants represented a variety of sexual orientations, with the majority (14 of 19) identifying as heterosexual. All had completed at least two years of graduate school and some were nearing dissertation defense and graduation. Relevant demographic information about each sorter is represented on the factor matrix of findings (see Table 1).

Instrument Development

The process of developing an instrument for Q methodology starts with the concourse (McKeown & Thomas, 2013) or the collection of all possible statements or items in response to the topic of study. We gathered more than 200 descriptors of stereotypes for non-monosexuality from informal discussions with graduate students, social media, and the queer literature. Then this large concourse was sampled, resulting in the Q set of 40 items to be sorted by participants. The sampling process was employed in two stages. First, all descriptors were gathered in groups

Table 1. Factor matrix showing demographics of sorters and defining sorter (X).

Sorter	Gender	Sexuality	Age	Race/Ethnicity	Factor A	Factor B
1	Male	Gay	32	Caucasian/White	.88X[a]	.32
3	Male	Gay	26	Caucasian/White	.76X[a]	.46
4	Male	Gay	40	Caucasian/White	.70X[a]	.36
5	Male	Heterosexual	25	Caucasian/White	.93X[a]	.18
6	Male	Heterosexual	28	Caucasian/White	.72X[a]	.46
7	Female	Heterosexual	27	Caucasian/White	.88X[a]	.29
8	Female	Heterosexual	23	Asian/Pacific Islander	.84X[a]	.23
9	Female	Heterosexual	26	Caucasian/White	.89X[a]	.30
10	Male	Heterosexual	29	Caucasian/White	.84X[a]	.40
13	Male	Heterosexual	35	Caucasian/White	.73X[a]	.30
19	Female	Heterosexual	27	Hispanic/Latina	.73X[a]	.49
14	Male	Gay	24	Caucasian/White	.37	.68X[a]
15	Male	Heterosexual	33	Caucasian/White	.03	.86X[a]
2	Female	Heteroflexible	26	Caucasian/White	.68	.62
11	Female	Heterosexual	30	Caucasian/White	.63	.58
12	Male	Heterosexual	27	Caucasian/White	.59	.55
16	Male	Heterosexual	33	Caucasian/White	.64	.61
17	Male	Heterosexual	25	Bi-Racial	.52	.63
18	Female	Heterosexual	38	African American	.58	.56
Percent explained variance					50	26
Number of defining sorts					11	2

[a]Original bold distinguished defining sorts.

because they were alike in some way, known as the homogeneous principle in Q methodology (Brown, 1980). We found three large groupings of descriptions. The general groupings related to personal and relational descriptors, those descriptors attributed by society or others, and another smaller group of stereotypes that were not specific to either category. Then, the principle of heterogeneity (Brown, 1980) was followed by choosing a sample of the different ideas within each of the groups. These two processes assured the greatest range of possible stereotypical descriptions of non-monosexuality were sampled from the concourse. The result of this sampling process was a Q set of 40 statements about the stereotypes associated with non-monosexuality.

With a Q set of 40 items, we determined the distribution for sorting to be along a continuum of 11 columns ranging from *most unlike* (−5) to *most like* (+5) requiring a forced distribution of 2, 3, 3, 4, 5, 6, 5, 4, 3, 3, 2 statements, respectively (see Figure 1). All 40 statements were descriptors printed on small cards and sorted by participants comparing one to another with the prompt, "What are your thoughts about individuals who are non-monosexual?" We provided examples of non-monosexual identities, that is, bisexual, pansexual, and queer, prior to the sort to ensure participants understood the concept. Standard sorting procedures were followed (Watts & Stenner, 2012). Specifically, we first instructed a brief reading of

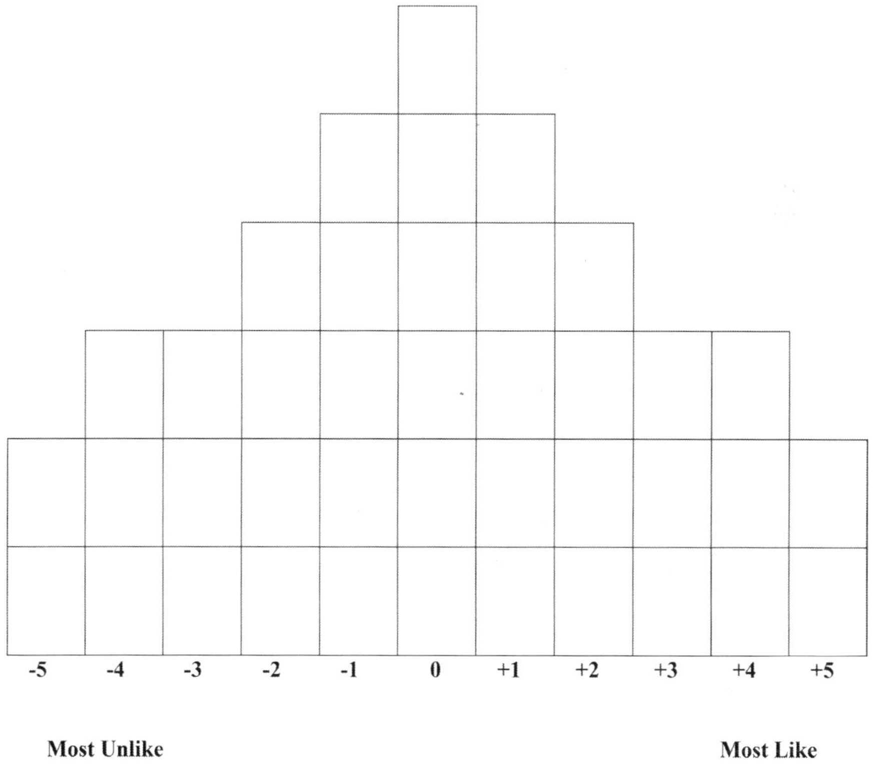

Figure 1. Record sheet for participant responses.

all descriptors and placing each in one of three general piles in front of the participant. The pile on the left would be descriptors the participants would feel is most unlike their thoughts, the pile on the right would be descriptors most like what they think about individuals who are non-monosexual, and the pile in the middle are those items to which they do not have any strong response. Then sorting proceeded by instructing participants to start with those descriptors with the strongest reactions and place the items in columns +5 (*most like*) and −5 (*most unlike*), then +4 and −4, and so forth until the sorting grid was filled with each item. Following the sorting procedure, each participant was asked to provide written feedback about the study and the descriptors they sorted, which most decided not to do. Participants completed a demographic questionnaire requesting information about gender, age, and sexual orientation.

Data Analysis

Q methodology consists of statistical analysis and interpretive analysis (Watts & Stenner, 2012). Statistical analysis includes correlation of each participants' entire sort to the 18 other participants' entire sorts, a factor analysis of the correlation matrix, and calculation of standard scores for the statements within each factor. Statistics were run using PQMethod, a commonly used free data analysis system for Q methodology (download from qmethod.org). Stephenson (1983) described the factor theory portion of Q methodology as analytical or explicatory; whereas, when factors are interpreted the complexity of meaning and understanding provides abductive discoveries. Interpretive analysis provides information and context to explain the statement arrangement within the stable factors and allows for application of findings (Brown, 1980).

When we examined the correlation matrix of sorts (indicating the relationship of all sorts to all other sorts), we were surprised by the similarity among the sorts. We first tried a centroid factor analysis and again noticed the strong one-factor solution. Without success in hand rotation to find sorts that clustered outside of the dominant axis, we then used a principal components factor analysis. With two factors having eigenvalues greater than one and the third unrotated factor with .87, we used varimax rotation on two factors to discern the variance in responses. These factor loadings (see Table 1) indicated a large one factor; however, with raising the significance level for establishing significant loads for sorts on factors another stable viewpoint emerged. The first factor was defined by 11 sorts and accounted for 50% of the explained variance, whereas the other factor was defined by two sorts and accounted for 26% of the explained variance. There were six confounding sorts that were not used to define the statements within the factor due to significant loading on both factors. Raising the significance level is similar to choosing sorts that most clearly represent the factor. This process allowed us to calculate the final statistical procedure and obtain standard scores (z-scores) for each statement within each of the two factors, resulting in the findings arrays.

We interpreted our factors using a combination of the z-score arrays for descriptors within factors, demographics of participants, and distinguishing and consensus statements across the two factors. We analyzed the z-score arrays within each factor to determine what descriptors within the Q set seemed to best represent the thoughts of the sorters who defined each factor. Distinguishing statements were those descriptors that differed between the two factor arrays and were significant at the .05 level or higher. Consensus statements were those descriptors that did not differ between the two factor arrays and were significant at the level of .01 or greater. We identified themes through analyzing groupings of descriptors to assist in naming each factor (Watts & Stenner, 2005, 2012). Consistent with interpretation strategies in Q methodology, we developed a likely narrative for each factor array based on the themes generated from the data (Wolf, 2004).

Findings

Based on our analysis of the data, two stable factors were found, "We're all Okay" and "You Might be Okay." (see Table 4 for array positions of each statement). Each factor is further explained herein through description of the participants that define the factor, themes found during interpretive analysis, and a narrative monologue of someone who may represent the factor. Only a single participant provided qualitative remarks on the study, which did not provide enough depth to contribute to factor development.

We're all Okay

The first factor was defined by 11 sorts and accounted for 50% of the variance. Three themes characterized "We're all Okay": (1) radical acceptance, (2) established identity, (3) growth fostering (see Table 2).

Table 2. Defining "We're all Okay".

Theme	Statement	Rank	z-Score
Radical acceptance	35. Deserve to be accepted	+5	1.895
	27. Contribute positively to their communities	+3	0.999
	15. Deserve to be shunned	−4	−1.558
	5. Are condemned to Hell	−5	−1.779
	4. Are sexual predators	−5	−1.821
Established identity	30. Are really confused	−2	−0.737
	31. Are actually gay or lesbian and haven't fully come out	−3	−0.931
	36. Are actually heterosexuals who are trying something different for the time being	−3	−0.935
	19. Are not real	−4	−1.560
Growth fostering	2. Are trustworthy	+4	1.358
	39. Are positive role models	+4	1.430
	16. Make good leaders	+3	1.002
	14. Can serve as religious leaders	+2	0.809
	29. Do not make satisfactory partners	−2	−0.915
	3. Do not make good parents	−3	−1.240

Radical acceptance appeared to characterize this view of non-monosexuality. These individuals seek to normalize attraction to multiple sexes or genders and seem to have a positive view of non-monosexuality. Participants that defined this viewpoint believed that non-monosexual people contribute positively (+3) to their communities and did not endorse controlling images, such as the ideas that non-monosexuals are "condemned to Hell" (−5) or "seem unhealthy and have more STIs" (−4).

Another theme emerging from the data for this viewpoint was an understanding of non-monosexuality as an established identity and not a phase before coming out as gay or lesbian (−3). These participants endorsed views that go against the view of non-monosexuality as a transitionary phase or as a confused state (−2). Also of importance was the view that non-monosexual people lead healthy lifestyles (+2), which is not a common message in society about this identity group.

We're all Okay seemed to believe that non-monosexuals are growth fostering for others. Participants believed non-monosexual people are trustworthy (+4), positive role models (4) who "contribute positively to their communities" (+3). This viewpoint was distinguished by the idea that non-monosexuals can foster growth for others through social acts, such as serving as religious leaders (+2), being faithful partners (−2), and raising children (−3). This theme represented a view that people who identify as non-monosexual cannot only be healthy and happy individually but also in a communal role.

A narrative the details the data and thematic analysis is as follows:

> I don't understand why people make a huge deal out of what someone's sexuality is. We all just want to love and be loved. People who are attracted to multiple sexes are no different. I actually know plenty of people who are non-monosexual and think they are great people. They have to deal with other people, gay people and heterosexual people, thinking poorly of their sexuality. I just don't get it. The people I know who are non-monosexual are just like everyone else and deserve to be happy and accepted.

"You Might be Okay"

Another view of the 19 participants was clearly defined by two sorts and accounted for 26% of the variance. Three themes that explain this factor include (1) mixed feelings, (2) tentative social recognition, (3) controlling images (see Table 3).

This viewpoint was characterized by participants endorsing ideas that seem to represent doubt regarding participant's views of non-monosexual people. For example, participants seem to question the visibility of the non-monosexual community. Participants felt non-monosexuals may "comprise a visible group of identities" (+1), but conversely may think they "typically comprise a silent community" (+2). Additionally, individuals who defined this factor thought people who are non-monosexual "have a solidified grasp on their sexuality" (+3) but also felt they "are indecisive about their sexual preference" (+1). These differing views seem to represent a certain uncertainty of non-monosexuality.

Table 3. Defining "You Might be Okay".

Theme	Statement	Rank	z-Score
Doubting	24. Seek a unified community	+5	1.747
	7. Have a solidified grasp on their sexuality	+3	1.215
	6. Typically comprise a silent community	+2	0.836
	10. Are indecisive about their sexual preference	+1	0.722
	26. Comprise a visible group of identities	+1	0.267
Tentative social recognition	35. Deserve to be accepted	+3	1.178
	13. Serve others in positive ways	+3	0.760
	27. Contribute positively to their communities	0	0.228
	2. Are trustworthy	0	−0.153
	39. Are positive role models	−2	−0.607
	16. Make good leaders	−2	−0.722
	14. Can serve as religious leaders	−4	−1.404
Endorsed stereotypes	37. Can often be more exploratory in their experiences	+5	1.178
	6. Typically comprise a silent community	+2	0.836
	10. Are indecisive about their sexual preference	+1	0.722
	27. Contribute positively to their community	0	0.228
	3. Do not make good parents	−1	−0.343
	21. Stay in long-term relationships	−1	−0.457
	14. Can serve as religious leaders	−4	−1.404

This group seemed to agree with the idea that non-monosexuals are often romantically/sexually involved with multiple people at a given time (+2), and also feeling like they may be indecisive about their sexual preferences (+1). These particular views are consistent with common stereotypes of non-monosexual people (Fox, 1991; Israel & Mohr, 2004). The second factor also highlighted questions about non-monosexual people's abilities to be good parents (−1) and stay in long-term relationships (−1). Individuals who defined this viewpoint also questioned non-monosexual people's roles as religious leaders (−4), representing the commonly held belief that LGBTQ+ individuals cannot also be religious.

A monologue that summarizes this viewpoint is as follows:

> I am hesitant when it comes to non-monosexual people. I believe they can be good people and accept who they are, but I'm not sure about how comfortable I am with it being a social norm. I have heard some negative things about them, and I'm not sure if I believe those things or not. I know some people who have identified this way, but some just end up calling themselves gay later on. I think non-monosexual people are fine interpersonally, and I trust them, but there are just some question marks around saying, "Oh, that's totally acceptable."

Commonalities between Factors

There were 24 consensus statements between the two factors. Consensus statements are statements in the Q set with z-scores that were not significantly different across factors (McKeown & Thomas, 2013). These consensus statements represented shared ideas between individuals across the two factors. For example, both individuals on both factors believed non-monosexual people "deserve to be accepted"(+5, +3) and do not "deserve to be shunned" (−4, −5), which has not always

Table 4. Data as array positions by statement.

Statement	"We're all Okay"	"I'm Okay, You Might be Okay"
1. Live swinger lifestyles	−1	−4
2. Are trustworthy	+4	0
3. Do not make good parents	−3	−1
4. Are sexual predators	−5	−3
5. Are condemned to Hell	−5	−1
6. Typically comprise a silent community	0	+2
7. Have a solidified grasp on their sexuality	+1	+3
8. Tend to be more accepting of others than their heterosexual, gay, and lesbian peers	0	+4
9. Make desirable romantic partners	+1	0
10. Are indecisive about their sexual preferences	−1	+1
11. Lead healthy lifestyles	+2	0
12. Are typically more open to other people	0	+3
13. Serve others in positive ways	+2	+2
14. Can serve as religious leaders	+2	−4
15. Deserve to be shunned	−4	−5
16. Make good leaders	+3	−2
17. Are often polyamorous or romantically involved with more than one person at a time	0	+2
18. Seem unhealthy and have more STIs	−4	0
19. Are not real	−4	−3
20. Are just experimenting with different sexes	−1	−1
21. Stay in long-term relationships	+3	−1
22. Are more likely to be unfaithful	−2	−5
23. Tend to be overly sexual	−1	+1
24. Seek a unified community	1	+5
25. Make desirable sexual partners	0	+1
26. Comprise a visible group of identities	1	+1
27. Contribute positively to their communities	+3	0
28. Are just as capable of monogamy as their heterosexual, gay, and lesbian peers	+4	+3
29. Do not make satisfactory partners	−2	−4
30. Are really confused	−2	−2
31. Are actually gay or lesbian and haven't fully come out	−3	0
32. Typically express their sexuality in a way that is congruent with their values	+1	+1
33. Have to be attracted to men and women equally	−2	−2
34. Are typically selfish lovers	−1	−1
35. Deserve to be accepted	+5	+3
36. Are actually heterosexual who are trying something different for the time being	−3	−3
37. Can often be more exploratory in their experiences	0	+5
38. Live happy lives	+5	+1
39. Are positive role models	+4	−2
40. Work hard to establish their identities	+2	+4

been a common cultural belief. Each factor represented acceptance in varied ways, with We're all Okay being radically accepting and You Might be Okay being individually accepting. Other stereotypes were not endorsed by either factor, such as the ideas that non-monosexual people "do not make satisfactory partners" (−2, −4) and that they "are not real" (−4, −3).

Consensus statements represented some stereotypes that have not been fully expunged, such as the idea that non-monosexuals are a silent community (0, 2) and that they are experimenting (−1, −1). Although none of these negative images was fully endorsed, factor arrays showed that these ideas fell toward the center of sorts for both factors. This placement could mean participants were unsure of these statements or that they may potentially be like non-monosexual people. Importantly, responses to more abrasive statements, such as "non-monosexuals are condemned to hell" (−5, −1) may not be endorsed due to current social expectations and feeling pressured by the researcher's presence. Having a researcher present while students sorted could have affected their responses and slanted sorts to be more positive and less pejorative.

Discussion

Our findings demonstrate shifting attitudes of graduate students' views toward non-monosexual identities. Prior research has demonstrated that non-monosexual people, specifically bisexual men, are often perceived less positively than their lesbian and gay counterparts (Parker, 2015). Our first factor clearly demonstrates a shift in views among our selection of graduate students. The strong first factor highlighted the message "We're All Okay," characterized by radical acceptance, seeing non-monosexuality as an established identity, and believing non-monosexuals to be growth-fostering members of communities. A second factor highlighted the message "You Might be Okay," characterized by doubt in interpretation of non-monosexuality, tentative social recognition, and endorsed stereotypes about non-monosexuality. Although society has grown more supportive of lesbian and gay identities over the past few decades, acceptance and specific services for non-monosexual identities have lagged behind (Pew Research Center, 2013), as demonstrated by our second factor.

We approached the application of these findings from a social justice and developmental perspective. Social justice inherently includes a value informed perspective of the findings (Rountree & Pomeroy, 2010). Developmental interpretation takes a prevention-oriented application, where intervention occurs early in the process of understanding and identifying with sexuality. The suggestions on how to apply these findings are oriented toward increasing recognition and acceptance of non-monosexuality. Specific suggestions for how graduate students can facilitate acceptance are also offered.

We propose that to expand the view that "we're all okay," we must provide support through community resources for those who are non-monosexual and those who support non-monosexual individuals. Previous research has demonstrated that community resources enhance the health of non-monosexual individual (Ebin, 2006), and those that define "We're All Okay" must be willing to assist non-monosexuals with accessing these resources. Support may take the form of actual support groups but may also include access to fact-based, person-centered resources and materials to provide people in their communities (van Lisdonk & Keuzenkamp, 2016). These materials would not continue to reaffirm stereotypes; rather they would reflect the uniqueness of non-monosexual identities and affirm diversity. Additionally, graduate students may be able to connect other students to

LGBTQ groups and educate LGBTQ groups on being inclusive of non-monosexual identities.

As was evidenced by "You Might be Okay," some graduate students are still tentative in their acceptance of people who are non-monosexual. This perception reflects the larger society, which is often biphobic (Friedman et al., 2014; Goodman, 2013). Although not inherently wrong in their views, these individuals appeared to be influenced by stereotypes that disenfranchise the non-monosexual community, such as the view that they cannot serve as religious. To potentially expand the tentative recognition, those who are fully accepting of non-monosexuality must continue to break down myths about the non-monosexual community.

Additionally, those who think non-monosexuals "might be okay" should be given the space to ask questions and gain knowledge in areas they may not understand. Graduate students can foster these discussions through intergroup dialogues, which bring together different social groups to make to discuss social problems, foster relationships, and create action toward social justice (Dessel, Rogge, & Garlington, 2006). These discussions have proven to help students develop better active listening skills, suspend their judgements, speak from their own perspective, and work constructively through conflict (Hopkins & Domingue, 2015). Intergroup dialogues on sexuality must include topics on negative stereotypes that affect the non-monosexual community, diverse definitions of non-monosexuality, and lived experiences. Graduate students can facilitate these discussions with their peers and undergraduates.

This study has limitations that could be accounted for in future research. Using non-monosexuality in our condition of instruction demonstrates that these attitudes apply to the umbrella of non-monosexual identities, moving beyond research only on bisexuality. When considering "non-monosexuality" as an umbrella term, we must acknowledge that many unique identities and experiences are represented. Future studies could ask participants about their perceptions of specific identity groups under the umbrella, which would provide more specific understandings of attitudes toward these individual groups. Additionally, given the perceived attention to diversity on college campuses, participants may have responded in socially desirable ways. Students who may have felt more negatively toward non-monosexuals may have chosen to restrict their true feelings because of the pressures of having a researcher present and because they do not wish to be perceived negatively. Despite the potential for socially desirable answers, our findings support the notion that more education often correlates to more acceptance of differences.

Finally, the most impactful limitations stem from the polarized Q set. The Q set was largely developed from prior research on stereotypes, which underemphasized experiential data and interpersonal interactions. Various participants commented on the black/white nature of the Q set, highlighting that some statements were clearly negative, whereas others were clearly positive, with few statements that would fall along a spectrum of viewpoints. This polarization affected the amount of confounding sorts and consensus statements, as the most positive and most negative statements, that is, "deserve to be shunned" and "deserve to be accepted," were sorted similarly across participants that defined different factors. Any future studies should develop a more balanced Q set that allows for more variability in responses and should address draw more statements from non-monosexuals' lived experiences.

More research is needed to address the needs of the non-monosexual community, with specific studies focusing on how their needs may be different than their gay and lesbian peers. We conducted this Q methodological study to begin filling that gap in the literature. Although this study has various limitations, the findings can be beneficial for creating more accepting environments for non-monosexual people. Graduate students can use these findings to encourage their peers and undergraduate students to challenge stereotypes and create accepting spaces for non-monosexual individuals. Through connecting non-monosexuals to resources, challenging stereotypes, and encouraging intergroup dialogues, graduate students can help create more accepting environments for non-monosexuals.

References

Barker, M., Richards, C., & Bowes-Catton, H. (2009). "All the world is queer save thee and me...": Defining queer and bi at a critical sexology seminar. *Journal of Bisexuality*, 9(3/4), 363–379. doi:http://dx.doi.org/10.1080/15299710903316638

Beemyn, G., & Rankin, S. (2011). Introduction to the special issue on "LGBTQ Campus Experiences." *Journal of Homosexuality*, *58*, 1159–1164. doi:10.1080/00918369.2011.605728

Bettinger, E. P., Long, B. T., & Taylor, E. S. (2016). When inputs are outputs: The case of graduate student instructors. *Economics of Education Review*, *52*, 63–76. doi:10.1016/j.econedurev.2016.01.005

Brown, S. R. (1980). *Political subjectivity: Applications of Q methodology in political science.* Newbury Park, CA: Sage.

Dentato, M. P. (2011). Minority stress predictors of substance use and sexual risk behavior among a cohort sample of men who have sex with men. Available from ProQuest Dissertations & Theses Full Text. Retrieved from http://ecommons.luc.edu/cgi/viewcontent.cgi?article=1249&context=luc_diss

Dessel, A., Rogge, M. E., & Garlington, S. B. (2006). Using intergroup dialogue to promote social justice and change. *Social Work, 51*(4), 303–315. doi:http://dx.doi.org.argo.library.okstate.edu/10.1080/10665684.2015.1057446

Ebin, J. (2006). Developing successful sexual health and support services for bisexual people: Lessons learned from the BiHealth program. *Journal of Bisexuality, 6*(1/2), 165–189. doi: http://dx.doi.org/10.1300/J159v06n01_09

Fox, A. (1991). Development of a bisexual identity: Understanding the process. In L. Hutchins & L. Kaahumanu (Eds.), *Bi any other name: Bisexual people speak out* (pp. 29–39). Boston, MA: Alyson.

Friedman, M. R., Dodge, B., Schick, V., Herbenick, D., Hubach, R. D., Bowling, J., ... Reece, M. (2014). From bias to bisexual health disparities: Attitudes toward bisexual men and women in the United States. *LGBT Health, 1*(4), 309–318. doi:10.1089/lgbt.2014.0005

Goodman, J. A. (2013, October 15). *Barriers to non-monosexual identities.* Retrieved from http://www.huffingtonpost.com/josh-a-goodman/barriers-to-non-monosexual-identities_b_4061334.html

Hoang, M., Holloway, J., & Mendoza, R. H. (2011). An empirical study into the relationship between bisexual identity congruence, internalized biphobia and infidelity among bisexual women. *Journal of Bisexuality, 11*(1), 23–38. doi:http://dx.doi.org.argo.library.okstate.edu/10.1080/15299716.2011.545285

Hong, J., Woodford, M., Long, L., & Renn, K. (2016). Ecological covariates of subtle and blatant heterosexist discrimination among LGBQ college students. *Journal of Youth and Adolescence, 45,* 117–131. doi:10.1007/s10964-015-0362-5

Hopkins, L. E., & Domingue, A. D. (2015). From awareness to action: College students' skill development in intergroup dialogue. *Equity & Excellence In Education, 48*(3), 392–402. doi: 10.1080/10665684.2015.1057446

Israel, T., & Mohr, J. J. (2004). *Attitudes toward bisexual women and men: Current research, future directions.* Binghamton, NY: Harrington Park Press/The Haworth Press.

Jorm, A. F., Korten, A. E., Rodgers, B., Jacomb, P. A., & Christensen, H. (2002). Sexual orientation and mental health: Results from a community survey of young and middle-aged adults. *British Journal of Psychiatry, 180*(5), 423–427. doi:10.1192/bjp.180.5.423

McKeown, B., & Thomas, D. (2013). *Q methodology* (2nd ed.). Thousand Oaks, CA: Sage.

Meyer, M. (2003). Looking toward the interSEXions: Examining bisexual and transgender identity formation from a dialectical theoretical perspective. *Journal of Bisexuality, 3*(3/4), 151–170. doi:10.1300/J159v03n03_11

Morgan, E. M., & Thompson, E. M. (2007). Young women's sexual experiences within same-sex friendships: Discovering and defining bisexual and bi-curious identity. *Journal of Bisexuality, 6*(3), 7–34. doi:http://dx.doi.org/10.1300/J159v06n03_02

Parker, K. (2015, February 20). *Among LGBT Americans, bisexuals stand out when it comes to identity, acceptance.* Retrieved from http://www.pewresearch.org/fact-tank/2015/02/20/among-lgbt-americans-bisexuals-stand-out-when-it-comes-to-identity-acceptance/

Pascarella, E. T., & Terenzini, P. T. (2005). *How college affects students: A third decade of research* (Vol. 2). San Francisco, CA: Jossey-Bass.

Pew Research Center. (2013). *A survey of LGBT Americans.* Retrieved from http://www.pewsocialtrends.org/2013/06/13/a-survey-of-lgbt-americans/

Pew Research Center. (2016). *A wider ideological gap between more and less educated adults.* Retrieved from http://www.people-press.org/2016/04/26/a-wider-ideological-gap-between-more-and-less-educated-adults/

Rankin, S., Weber, G., Blumenfeld, W., & Frazer, S. (2010). *2010 state of higher education for lesbian, gay, bisexual and transgender people.* Charlotte, NC: Campus Pride.

Rountree, M. A., & Pomeroy, E. C. (2010). Bridging the gaps among social justice, research, and practice. *Social Work, 55*(4), 293–295. doi:10.1093/sw/55.4.293

Stephenson, W. (1953). *The study of behavior; Q-technique and its methodology.* Chicago, IL: University of Chicago Press. Retrieved from http://argo.library.okstate.edu/login?url=http://search.proquest.com.argo.library.okstate.edu/docview/615262244?accountid=4117

Stephenson, W. (1973). Applications of communication theory III-intelligence and multivalued choice. *The Psychological Record, 23*(1), 17–32.

Stephenson, W. (1980). Newton's fifth rule and Q methodology: Application to educational psychology. *American Psychologist, 35,* 882–889. doi:10.1037/0003-066X.35.10.882

Stephenson, W. (1983). Quantum theory and Q-methodology: Fictionalistic and probabilistic theories conjoined. *Psychological Record, 33*(2), 213–230.

van Lisdonk, J., & Keuzenkamp, S. (2016). Towards bi-inclusive policies: Suggestions based on research on Dutch same-sex attracted young people. *Sexuality Research & Social Policy: A Journal of the NSRC,* doi:10.1007/s13178-016-0241-1

Watts, S., & Stenner, P. (2005). Doing Q methodology: Theory, method and interpretation. *Qualitative Research in Psychology, 2*(1), 67–91. doi:http://dx.doi.org.argo.library.okstate.edu/10.1191/1478088705qp022oa

Watts, S., & Stenner, P. (2012). *Doing Q methodological research: Theory, method, and interpretation.* Thousand Oaks, CA: Sage.

Wolf, A. (2004). *Operant Subjectivity, 27,* 145–165.

Woodford, M. R., Kulick, A., Sinco, B. R., & Hong, J. S. (2014). Contemporary heterosexism on campus and psychological distress among LGBQ students: The mediating role of self acceptance. *American Journal of Orthopsychiatry, 84,* 519–529. doi:10.1037/ort0000015

"It's not Pans, It's People": Student and Teacher Perspectives on Bisexuality and Pansexuality

Alicia Anne Lapointe

ABSTRACT

This article explores how Canadian youth who participate in Gay-Straight Alliances (GSA) and teachers who advise them perceive and/or experience bi/pansexuality. Participants' perspectives on, definitions of, and alignment with bi/pansexuality are examined as they unpack mis/understandings associated with nonmonosexual identities. For GSA members, bisexual and pansexual identity labels were not interchangeable terms; bisexuality was associated with the fe/male binary and pansexuality served as a personal contestation to this dichotomy. Despite these distinctions, both nonmonosexualities were marked by invisibility, mis/understandings, and prejudice in school. Findings emphasize how students' knowledge of sexual diversity and fluidity was more nuanced than their GSA advisors due to personal online research. GSA participation enabled bi/pansexual knowledge exchange among students and teachers, and promoted overall understandings of bi/pansexualities. Although GSA involvement facilitated opportunities to discuss bi/pansexualities, this article also highlights how an effort should be made to integrate bi/pansexual content in these clubs.

This article examines how Canadian youth who participate in Gay-Straight Alliances (GSA) and teachers who advise them in four publically funded Ontario high schools perceive and/or experience bi/pansexualities. Participants' perspectives on, definitions of, and alignment with bisexuality and pansexuality are explored as they unpack mis/understandings associated with nonmonosexual identities. Stigma and resilience among bi/pansexual people are examined with particular attention being paid to youth's experiences with biphobic prejudice— negative attitudes toward bisexuality (Taylor et al., 2015; Weiss, 2003) and misunderstandings related to their identification as pansexual. The findings are particularly salient considering there is little scholarship that explores bi/pansexualities in schooling (Elia, 2014; McAllum, 2014) and an increasing amount of youth who identify beyond the homo/heterosexual binary (Pallotta-Chiarolli, 2010; Lapointe, in press-b). Because monosexuality is privileged over bi/pansexualities in society (Roberts, Horne, & Hoyt, 2015), bi/pansexual youth, like trans folks, often assume the role of cultural workers who actively de/re/construct gender (Elia, 2010), and subsequently sexuality through identifications that transgress fe/male and hetero/homo classification (Callis, 2014).

'Pansexuality' is commonly defined as the potential to be attracted to people of any gender identity (Kosciw, Greytak, Palmer, & Boesen, 2014; Taylor et al., 2015), whereas bisexuality is positioned as an attraction to males and females (Kosciw et al., 2014). However, like any sexual identity, there is no universally-correct definition of 'bisexuality' (see Sullivan, 2003). For example, some bisexual people are attracted to two specific genders, such as women and genderqueer folks, which debunks the myth that bisexuality is rooted in the fe/male binary. As such, it is important to note that Kosciw et al.'s (2014) definition of 'bisexuality' is widely contested. Walkley and Kinsey (2013) assert:

> The idea that bisexuals are attracted to only two genders is an incredibly common stereotype of all bisexuals. Many people assume that the "bi" aspect of the word "bisexuality" implies a gender binary, and that those who identify as bisexual are only attracted to males and females. Though there are definitely bisexual individuals who are only attracted to cisgender people with male and female gender identities, there are also bisexuals who are attracted to people who are transgender, intersex, genderqueer and more; this assumed definition of "bisexual" leaves out those of us who are attracted to gender-non-conforming people—those who fall outside the "male" and "female" ends of an incredibly wide gender spectrum.

Despite growing knowledges that problematize limited understandings of bisexuality, Taylor et al. (2015) write that some people identify "as 'pansexual' rather than 'bisexual' to recognize the[ir] potential for attraction to sexes and/or genders that exist across a spectrum and to challenge the sex/gender binary" (p. 5; see also Autumn, 2013; Callis, 2014). Following this line of thought, this study explores students' understanding and embracement of pansexual identification over bisexuality, as well as the erasure of bi/pansexualities in Canadian secondary schools.

Because formal schooling lacks curricular inclusions that espouse respect and dignity for sexual and gender minorities (SGM) (Taylor et al., 2011; see also Lapointe, 2014, 2015b), and the erasure of bi/pansexualities in formal curriculum is well documented (Elia, 2010, 2014), participants' understandings of bi/pansexualities was enhanced by personal online research, and participation in their school's GSA. Although, the name 'GSA' "seems problematic in that 'gay' does not necessarily refer to lesbians or bisexuals and trans identities … the acronym "GSA" [has come] to represent any student group concerned with LGBTQ [lesbian, gay, bisexual, queer/questioning] matters" (Taylor et al., 2011, p. 19; see also Elia, 2010, 2014). The following research questions are answered throughout this article to provide a more nuanced overview of bi/pansexual identification and oppression in four Canadian high schools: How are GSA members and teacher advisors identifying with and/or describing bi/pansexualities? What challenges do bi/pansexual students face and how are they addressing these challenges? How are students and advisors learning about bi/pansexualities?

Theory

Queer theoretical perspectives

Queer perspectives underpin the study's conceptualization, execution, and data analysis (see Linville, 2009). In contrast to hetero/cisnormative understandings of sexuality and gender, which position identities as fixed, stable, and dichotomous (Sullivan, 2003), this study recognizes and affirms the fluid, spectral, and nonessentialist identities and expressions of SGMs (see Grace & Wells, 2015). Although, as Sears (2014) writes, sociocultural prejudice has propagated a bifurcated understanding of sexuality, Carlson (2014) asserts that knowledge of sexuality and gender is moving beyond rigid binarized categorizations of homosexual/heterosexual and fe/male. Thus, queer theory is employed to problematize "the understanding of subjects in terms of fixed and stable binary identities that implicate subjects in categories that are hierarchical, patriarchal, and unequal.." (Ruffolo, 2006). Drawing on queer perspectives, this article explores youth's personal (and sometimes fluid) identifications with bi/pansexuality, and their experiences with heteronormativity and monosexism in the education system.

Identity construction

Britzman (1997) contends that identities, such as those involving expressions of and adherence to heterosexuality, are constructed and thus, "*No* sexual identity, even the most normative, is automatic, authentic, easily assumed, or without negotiation and construction" (p. 186). Her writing interrogates the claim that heterosexuality is a natural and normal sexual expression; instead, asserting that every identity is negotiated and constituted under social and political conditions, within particular histories (Britzman, 1995, 1997, 1998). Bi/pansexualities are no different in that youth re/de/construct their nonmonosexual identities throughout various times, places, and spaces (Callis, 2014). Likewise, Butler (1990) contends that gender and sexual categories (e.g., gay and woman) are social constructs that are affected by sociocultural histories and politics. Butler suggests that a map of cultural understanding—the heterosexual matrix—exists whereby bodies, genders, and desires are read as 'natural' in society. For Butler, sex, gender, and sexuality are mutual and reinforcing concepts whereby bodies and desires become intelligible when "a stable sex [is] expressed through a stable gender … that is oppositionally and hierarchically defined though the compulsory practice of heterosexuality" (p. 206). The heterosexual matrix normalizes the male/female binary and assigns, for example, a feminine gender to a 'female' body to which a physical and romantic desire for males are imposed.

The concept of a stable and predictable sexual orientation and gender are rooted in scientific/medical knowledge claims that position people as either male or female; this supposedly determines their gender as masculine or feminine and consequently their hetero/sexuality (Butler, 1990). Trans identities and expressions are not commonly acknowledged, accepted, or affirmed in schools (Grace & Wells, 2015; Kosciw et al., 2014; Taylor et al., 2015; Taylor et al., 2011; Wyss, 2004) because they deviate from the fe/male categories that have become 'normal' and 'natural' (see Butler, 1990; Callis, 2014); thus, "Non-binary identities such as ... pansexual provide a critical site for the investigation of how sexual identity is both constructed and de/reconstructed" (Callis, 2014, pp. 63–64). Through this article it is argued that nonbinary terms, such as trans and genderqueer lack mainstream currency (Grace & Wells, 2015), and this absence contributes to pansexual invisibility and prejudice. "Although bisexuality has broken some of these dichotomies [homo/heterosexual], other sexual identities, specifically pansexuality ... continue to break down dichotomies of gender, sexual identity, and sexual orientation" (Autumn, 2013, p. 329). Pansexuality, as defined and expressed by youth, serves as a political contestation to the fe/male dichotomy, and an opening to acknowledge and embrace non-binary sexualities and experiences.

Literature review

Safety and support for bi/pansexual students

Grace and Wells (2015) assert, "Historically, schools have been expected to replicate the status quo in which heteronormativity and genderism are driving cultural forces" (p. 117; see also Elia, 2014); these prejudicial ideologies give rise to homo/bi/transphobic prejudice and discrimination in American and Canadian secondary schools (see Kosciw et al., 2014; Kosciw et al., 2012; Taylor et al, 2011; Walton, 2006). Within a Canadian context, Egale Canada Human Rights Trust, a SGM human rights organization, administered the first national climate survey on homo/bi/transphobia in Canadian schools. Survey results from more than 3,700 students indicated that 64% of SGM youth felt unsafe at school (Taylor et al., 2011). Of these youth, 75% of female bisexual youth and 51% of male bisexual youth felt unsafe at school, with 63% of female bisexual youth and 39% of male bisexual voicing that their sexuality negatively affected their safety (Taylor et al., 2011). In the United States, 71.4% of students frequently heard 'gay' used inappropriately (e.g., "that's so gay"), and 90.8% of youth were distressed by this language (Kosciw et al., 2014). Additionally, 64.5% of students reported frequently hearing other homophobic language (e.g., "dyke" and "faggot") (Kosciw et al., 2014).

Fifty-six percent of female bisexual youth and 37% of male bisexual youth have had mean rumors or lies spread about their sexuality compared to 52% of lesbian and 47% of gay male youth (Taylor et al., 2011). In addition, 43% of Canadian, female bisexual students experience sexual harassment, and 26% of female and 12% of male bisexual youth have been physically harassed (Taylor et al., 2011). It is significant to note that oppression across the sexuality spectrum is not uniform, with people who identify under the bisexual umbrella facing prejudice and discrimination from outside and within queer/trans communities (Mitchell, Davis, & Galupo, 2015). Recent research has also found that people who identity as bisexual report more discrimination from heterosexual people than gay and lesbian folks (Roberts et al., 2015); these findings paired with the alarming rates of sexual, physical, and verbal violence directed at bisexual youth (see Kosciw et al., 2014; Taylor et al., 2011), call for formal education to integrate positive content on bi/pansexualities and address bi/panphobia in schooling.

Sexual and gender minority-inclusive curriculum

Although 85% of Canadian educators approve of SGM-inclusive education. (Taylor et al., 2015), Taylor et al.'s (2011) research reveal that few school boards provide teachers with SGM-inclusive educational resources or encourage educators to address homo/bi/transphobia through school curriculum. Despite inadequate SGM resources, training, and administrative support, three fourths of participants in Taylor et al.'s (2015) study reported that they had included SGM content in their teaching. Educators, however, most often challenged homophobia and used inclusive language/examples, rather than acknowledging and affirming bi/pansexualities, or problematizing the homo/hetero and male/female binaries. Lacklustre training and resources prevent many educators from addressing SGM issues, particularly in Catholic schools (Taylor et al., 2015), and highlight a need for "greater understanding of bisexuality and sexual diversity … through preservice training and professional development (McAllum, 2014, p. 87), as well as personal online research (Lapointe, 2015a). In addition to formal professional development and self-directed learning, educators can learn from and with youth who are members of GSAs (Lapointe, 2015a).

Queering education via gay-straight alliances

GSAs have been endorsed through provincial government policy because these school-based clubs are effective in promoting safer spaces for SGM youth and reducing homophobic bullying and harassment in schools (Kitchen & Bellini, 2013). In addition to providing much needed safety and support for SGM youth (see Liboro, Travers, & St. John, 2015), GSAs may also adopt a queer pedagogical agenda when club members engage in non-normative discussions involving SGM issues (Lapointe, 2014; Miceli, 2005). When clubs focus on education, they may provide youth with their only opportunity to interrogate stereotypes;, address mis/understandings; rethink prejudicial attitudes and beliefs; share stories of gender, sexual, and romantic minority (GSRM)-based marginalization and resilience; and address heteronormativity (Conway & Crawford-Fisher, 2007; Lapointe, 2014). GSAs can provide anti-homo/biphobic education (Elliott, 2015; Lapointe, 2014, 2015a, 2015b; Mayo, 2013), help their members confront injustice and lobby for social change (Conway & Crawford-Fisher, 2007; Currie, Mayberry, & Chenneville, 2012; Elliott, 2015; Mayo, 2013, 2015; Russell, Muraco, Subramaniam, & Laub, 2009), and encourage students to challenge heterosexism and heteronormativity (Garcia-Alonso, 2004; see also Lapointe, 2014, 2015a, 2015b). GSA's educative role may compensate for an absence of SGM-inclusive curriculum (Lapointe, 2015a) and as this study will demonstrate provide an outlet to explore bi/pansexualities and problematize bi/panphobic attitudes and beliefs.

Method

Case study research allows a researcher to "..focus on a 'case' and retain a holistic and real-world perspective.." (Yin, 2014, p. 4) using specific data collection, organization, and analysis methods (Patton, 2002). For this multiple, embedded case study the unit of analysis was GSAs: two high school clubs located in two different Ontario, Catholic school boards, and two groups within one Ontario, public school board. The findings in this article reflect a subset of data from a larger study, which examined the roles and purposes of GSAs in Ontario Catholic and public high schools. The total sum of data was collected over a 5-month period, from March 2015 through July 2015 and included data from observing each of the four GSAs in action, conducting 19 interviews (five advisors, 14 students, and one activist who challenged the banning of GSAs in Ontario Catholic schools); receiving bi/weekly semistructured diaries from 14 students; and analyzing visual materials produced by each club. Data collection included a variety of methods to increase the validity of findings (Patton, 2002; Yin, 2009). For the purpose of this article, data derived from participant observation (i.e., March 2015 through June 2015), 10 interviews (i.e., two advisors and eight students); four semistructured student diaries; and a video created by one GSA and a PowerPoint developed by another were the methodological tools that were used to produce knowledge on bi/pansexualities within an educational context (see Elia, 2014). Through data analysis, bi/pansexuality emerged as smaller theme; thus, only interviews, diaries, and visual data sources that explicitly explored bi/pansexualities from the vantage point of GSA members and advisors were analyzed for the purpose of this article.

Case and participant recruitment

To acquire GSA cases and student and teacher participants an e-mail invitation was sent to secondary school principals in three southwestern Ontario school boards. Interested schools were asked to reply to the researcher via e-mail. The researcher then visited interested clubs to inform GSA members and advisors about the nature of the study and offer them an opportunity to participate. For the researcher to observe and participate in GSA meetings all student members and advisors had to provide informed consent. Before the researcher could commence participant observation, all consent forms had to be completed and returned.

Informed consent and participants

GSA members, age 18 years or older, and advisors were asked to sign a letter of consent where they could select whether or not they (1) consented to the researcher's presence and participation at GSA meetings/events, (2) agreed to be interviewed, and (3) agreed to have their interview audio-recorded. Youth were also given an additional option of completing bi/weekly semistructured diaries. Students younger than age 18 were required to have their guardian(s) sign a letter of assent, which authorized their involvement in the study. If students had not disclosed their SGM status to their guardian(s) and they are unable or unwilling to 'out' themselves due to safety concerns, they did not have to receive permission from their guardian(s) to participate in the study. Instead, they were permitted to sign a waiver form and consent to their own participation. This exception was approved by the Western University Research Ethics Board and the three school boards that participated in the study. The waiver inclusion aligns with many Ontario anti-homo/transphobic school board policies that protect students from being 'outed' to their guardian(s), specifically if it could compromise their safety. Please refer to Table 1 for a summary of participants. All student, teacher, and school names are pseudonyms to protect participant confidentiality.

Participant observation

Participant observation provided insight into GSA members' and advisors' interpersonal behaviors and motives (Yin, 2014). The researcher observed participants in a variety of social contexts, such as internal group activities (e.g., GSA meetings, club socials, GSA social media sites, etc.), and school-wide initiatives and events

Table 1. Summary of participants.

Participant	Role	School[a]	Sexual Orientation	Gender Identity	Individual Data Collection Method(s)[b]
Taylor	Student	Blessed Sacrament	"Straight"	"Female"	Interview
Skylar	Student	Sunset High	"Pansexual"	"Female"	Interview
Andie	Student	Village High	Label-less	"Male"	Semistructured diaries
Hayden	Student	Village High	"Pansexual"	"Male" and "Genderfluid"	Interview
Sasha	Student	Village High	"Asexual"	"Male"	Interview
Reese	Student	Village High	"Pansexual" ("prefer cisgender women")	"Demiboi"	Interview; Semistructured diaries;
Hunter	Student	Holy Names	"Probably Pansexual" (prefer females)	"Transguy"	Interview
Kai	Student	Village High	"Gay"	"Nonbinary"	Interview
Azariah	Student	Blessed Sacrament	"Straight"	"Female"	Interview
Peyton	Student	Holy Names	"Lesbian"	"Female"	Semistructured diaries
Blake	Student	Sunset High	Did not disclose	Did not disclose	Semistructured diaries
Dylan	Teacher	Village High	"Gay"	"Female"	Interview
Zion	Teacher	Sunset High	"Straight"	"Female"	Interview

[a] Only data collection methods(s) utilized for this purpose of this article are depicted in Table 1.
[b] The four schools in this study are publically-funded institutions. Village High and Sunset High are nondenominational and Holy Names and Blessed Sacrament are Catholic schools.

(e.g., assemblies, movie nights, etc.). The researcher acted as a participant in group discussions and activities, taking on a full membership role in the GSA. During GSA meetings/events, participants' actions and behaviors were documented as well as the researcher's subjective interpretations of GSA initiatives, activities, and events. These field notes provided significant opportunities to engage in rich analysis (Saldana, 2013). Because the researcher was an active participant in the GSA rather than a passive observer, it is important to acknowledge that this may have caused GSA members and advisors to act in socially-desirable ways.

Semistructured interviews

One hour semistructured interviews with GSA members and teacher advisors allowed participants to discuss content and events that they felt were meaningful, and encouraged them to "..express their own understandings [about bi/pansexualities] in their own terms" (Patton, 2002, p. 348). Interviews helped explain behavioral events and provide insight into personal views (e.g., experiences, opinions, attitudes, and meanings associated with bi/pansexualities) (see Yin, 2014). Interviews with consenting participants were audio-recorded and transcribed. Interview transcriptions were cross-referenced with observational notes, and semistructured diaries to verify the main findings (Yin, 2014).

Semistructured diaries

Consenting students were asked to complete bi/weekly semistructured diaries to examine their actions, behaviors, feelings, attitudes, and learnings associated with club membership and participation. After each GSA meeting youth from each GSA were asked to respond to one question developed by the researcher via e-mail. The researcher developed the diary questions after each GSA meeting. Questions focused on learning associated with club participation—as per the primary purpose of the study. As such, the researcher inquired about participants' perspectives on and experiences with GSA discussions, activities, and events. Sample questions include "Have you learned anything new from participating in GSA? If so, what was it? Have you had an opportunity to share any lesbian, gay, bisexual, trans, two-spirit, queer/questioning, intersex, asexual (LGBT2QIA)-related information with your group (e.g., social media, news article, app, resource, community event, etc.)? What are some characteristics that make a teacher a great GSA advisor?" Similar to the observation limitations listed above, the researcher acknowledges that diary questions could have impacted the content of future meetings.

Visual materials

Visual images, such as videos, PowerPoint presentations, displays, posters, signs, and images that the group created as a part of their club activities, initiatives, or events were analyzed to provide insight into the cultural features and functional components of GSAs (see Yin, 2014). Through informal interactions, interviews, and diaries, the researcher elicited participants' reflections on the visual materials and inquired about their meaning (Saldana, 2013). Analytic insights were documented through field notes and analytic memos to generate language-based data to correspond to GSA-developed visuals (see Saldana, 2013).

Data analysis

Thematic analysis was employed to distill key patterns within the data. Throughout data collection the researcher wrote down preliminary words/phrases for potential codes on field notes, documents, or within analytic memos (Patton, 2002; Saldana, 2013). A codebook—a record of emergent codes, their descriptions, and examples—was developed and referenced during first- and second-cycle data analysis (Saldana, 2013). All data that contained participant activities and their perceptions, transcripts, artifacts, analytic memos, and observational field notes were encoded with (1) attribute, (2) descriptive, (3) in vivo, (4) process, and (5) values first cycle coding methods (Saldana, 2013). After primary codes were applied coded data was reviewed and reworked using second-cycle coding methods; this process helped the researcher categorize information, detect patterns, generate themes/concepts, and build theory (Saldana, 2013). For this process the researcher placed similar codes together to determine their commonalities and created an overarching pattern code. These codes were used to develop statements that illustrated major themes and a relationship network across the data (Saldana, 2013).

Results

Thinking beyond LGBT identifications: Youth's gravitation toward pansexuality

In contrast to Mitchell et al.'s (2015) study with 235 participants where 43.4% of people identified as bisexual and 28.9% identified as pansexual, the four participants in this study, who currently expressed multiple gender attraction, identified as pansexual (see also Rust, 2001). Student participants aligned themselves with pansexuality to affirm and express their authentic sexuality, and to problematize the restrictive fe/male binary (see Butler, 1990; Callis, 2014). Only one participant occasionally identified as bisexual to help others, who were unfamiliar with the term 'pansexual,' understand her nonmonosexual sexuality. Although 'bisexuality' and 'pansexuality' are arguably similar in terms of people experiencing sexual attraction to more than one gender (see Walkley & Kinsey, 2013), participants preferred 'pansexual' as an identity label because, as Autumn (2013) and Callis (2014) claim, it tends to be more inclusive of trans people. As was the case in Savin-Williams' (2005) and Ghaziani's (2011, 2014) empirical work, nonmonosexual youth in this study did not align their sexual orientation with preexisting lesbian, gay, bisexual, transgender (LGBT) identification categories per see (see also

Lapointe, in press-b); instead, pansexuality was purposefully employed to dismantle the homo/heterosexual and fe/male binaries and affirm the spectral nature of sexuality and gender (see Butler, 1990; see also Grace & Wells, 2015). Unlike many of their peers and teachers, participants who previously or currently identified as pansexual had a more nuanced understanding of bi/pansexualities and purposefully selected this lesser known term to represent their true sexuality (see also Lapointe, in press-b).

"Is it pans"?: Confusion regarding the term 'pansexual'

Sasha communicated that most of the students who came out from his elementary school were "pan or bisexual...," which demonstrates how many youth are subverting the homo/heterosexual binary (Pallotta-Chiarolli, 2010). Skylar, Hayden, Reese, and Hunter self-identified as pansexual. Sasha and Kai previously identified as pansexual yet at the time of their interviews identified as asexual and gay, respectively, which spotlights the fluid and spectral nature of sexuality (see Britzman, 1995; Ruffolo, 2006). Hunter expressed that his sexuality confused people, likely because fluidity, as Ruffolo (2006) states, "problematizes the understanding of subjects in terms of fixed and stable binary identities." Hunter stated that people did not understand his current sexual identification label, especially because it was in-flux:

> Sexual orientation has been kind of hard just because it tends to be a little all over the place and it's a little more fluid than I would prefer; just because I mean telling someone one thing and then several months later it's a little bit different and I think it confuses people. But its yeah it's just I'm probably pan with a preference toward females but a lot of people are like 'what'?

Like Hunter, Skylar had to endure confusion from others when she disclosed her sexual orientation. She also felt compelled to deconstruct prejudicial assumptions about what someone who is pansexual is supposed to look like. She declared

> ...literally, every time I tell somebody, "Oh, yeah, I date girls and guys and whoever else in between." They're like, "What?" It surprises them because they're like, "You don't look like the type." I'm like, "Do I have to look like a type? I'm me. I don't have to be a type."

Not only did Skylar have to refute stereotypical assumptions about her sexuality, she was consistently expected to educate others about her pansexual identity (see Kumashiro, 2002). She asserts, "I've had people ask me what my sexuality means. 'Gee, I think it sounds obvious. But, if it's not, let me tell you.'" Hunter, Skylar, and Hayden all agree that most people do not understand what pansexuality is, and Skylar and Hayden communicated that people think 'pan' is kitchenware. Hayden joked, "Is it pans?" To avoid confusion and questions, Skylar sometimes identified as bisexual. She stated:

> My sexual orientation is pansexual, though I do identify as bisexual. It's easier to explain bisexual to most people than pansexual because they automatically think you're kitchenware. But unfortunately for them, it's not pans, it's people.

Skylar believed that most people 'understood' the term 'bisexual'—probably because it is rooted in the fe/male binary (see Callis, 2014; Taylor et al., 2015); however, pansexuality appeared to be less obvious and even strange, demonstrating a cultural prejudice toward sexual duality (Sears, 2014). The researcher probed further, "So you're saying that sometimes it's easier just to tell people that you're bisexual?" to which Skylar answered:

> Yeah. Because some people, they don't understand what pan is. So, if you say you're pan, they're [the general public] going to be like, "What?" But if you say you're bi, they're like, "Oh, so you like both genders." And usually from there, I go off and I say like, "Okay, I will date transgender."

Skylar, like all student participants, acknowledged the spectral nature of gender (Grace & Wells, 2015), which influenced her journey toward identifying as pansexual, rather than bisexual (see Autumn, 2013).

'Oh, it's just a phase": Prejudicial attitudes toward bi/pansexualities

Besides encountering confusion, some students also experienced prejudice when they came out as bi/pansexual. Reese stated that when they initially identified as bisexual some of their sexual minority friends voiced prejudicial beliefs about bisexuality:

> when I was younger, I thought that I was bisexual. When I came out to my friends who are openly gay or openly lesbian, they just kind of laughed at me and said, "oh, it's just a phase." And I'm like, "but ... but it's not."... and even if it was, who are you to tell me that what I'm feeling is wrong and that it doesn't exist? The community is supposed to be open.

Similar to recent empirical work that highlights the pervasiveness of biphobic prejudice (Craig, McInroy, McCready, & Alaggia, 2015), these comments intended to invalidate Reese's nonmonosexual sexuality. Reese's experience demonstrates how biphobia also manifests in queer circles (see Roberts et al., 2015). They went on to acknowledge that SGM communities can be places where bi/pansexualities are not accepted to the same extent that monosexuality is:

> It's that one safe space [community] that we should all have, but not everybody has. Especially going back to the LGBT thing with the bisexuality, I think that's supposed to be your safe place. You know, talking to other community members that's supposed to be a safe place for you, that's supposed to help you. And I think when people act like that it's just—it's the opposite of what you need happening. I mean who are you to advocate against homophobia when you don't believe that a certain identity [bisexuality] exists, and openly vie against it.

Even Sasha, a SGM-knowledgeable individual, expressed hetero/cisnormative assumptions when he declared, "More people are straight. And when you have someone who's bi, that still counts as partially straight and partially gay so you still have that chance of a straight relationship happening." This harmful association positions bisexuality as inherently linked to the (false) gender binary and privileges a relationship status, rather than a person's self-affirmed identity, as their authentic sexual orientation.

It was apparent that, though they tend to be more educated than the general public, many student and teacher participants held prejudicial attitudes and assumptions about bi/pansexualities. For example, when asked the question, "What do you believe it's like to be a student who is LGBT2Q at your school"? Dylan, the advisor from Village High, stated:

> Depends on which letter they identify as because … I think the females, the ones who identify as female and who identify as either lesbian or bisexual, I think it's very easy for them. I think as of late, this sounds awful but I don't mean it in the rude way…. It seems like bisexuals and lesbianism is like a fad that the teenagers are going through. Like, "oh I can date anybody." Even though I know that's not the case, I think people are just more open and going, "oh it's more fluid."

As opposed to Taylor et al.'s (2011) findings, which debunk the notion that lesbianism is tolerated more than homosexuality and that lesbianism and bisexuality in females is trendy, Dylan believed that being bisexual in high school was somewhat easy. It appeared as if Skylar was speaking back to this teacher when she declared:

> As being somebody who is pansexual at a school where the population seems to be mostly straight, I would have to admit, I'm kind of ballsy for being as open as I am about it. And at first, I was afraid when I was younger because I didn't quite understand what it meant to be who I am. And as I discovered who I am, then I realized just how much opposition you get.

Pansexuality defined (by youth)

To dispel bi/pansexuality myths, and help combat confusion and bi/panphobic prejudice, this section explores how youth define and experience their pansexuality. It pays particular attention to debunking essentialist notions of identity (see Carlson, 2014). Despite the prevalence bi/pan phobia in schools and society (Elia, 2014; Pallotta-Chiarolli, 2010), participants affirmed their sexualities and celebrated their non-monosexual identities. For example, at a board-wide GSA conference a guest entertainer asked students to share why they joined the GSA at their school; one student declared, "I am openly bi and I don't care what people say!" This empowering GSA-specific experience demonstrated how, "For many students, the GSA is the space where self-discovery and validation of one's truest self may occur" (Mayo, 2015, p. 89).

When asked to describe what' pansexuality' meant to her, Skylar stated, "It doesn't matter what they have, like their body. It's their heart that matters … if they're cis, if they're not, it's just them." Skylar's assertion describes gender beyond the fe/male binary in that trans identities and expressions are acknowledged (Autumn, 2013; Kosciw et al., 2014); this was, for most youth in this study, a particularly salient aspect of pansexuality (Taylor et al., 2015). For Sasha, the acknowledgement of gender beyond the binary was paramount in determining his previously used sexual identity label, "For the longest time, I identified as pansexual … when I first learned about it [sexuality], I was like, oh maybe I'm bisexual … but, I prefer pansexual because … the two gender thing." Sasha preferred the term 'pansexuality' because gender was marked by possibilities, rather than prescription (Lapointe, in press-a). For Hayden, pansexuality involved the potential to be attracted to any human regardless of their intersecting identities:

> I know some people think it means boy, girl, in between, but the way I see it, it's kind of more like, it goes deeper than that. Not only it gender or sex or like race, religion, physical ability. I don't know it's just kind of you don't discriminate against anyone in particular. Like some people would be like, "oh I won't date this person because they're white or this person because they're black or this person because their Muslim," but I don't care about that.

Bi/pansexual learning via gay-straight alliances

GSAs can be sites where bi/pansexual learning takes place and shape. For example, the GSA at Blake, Skylar, and Zion's school brainstormed ideas for a GSA-led professional development session with Sunset High educators. The ideas they generated were incorporated into a PowerPoint presentation, which was constructed by Zion—the advisor, but delivered by Skylar. At the beginning of the session Skylar defined the lesbian, gay, bisexual, transgender, transsexual, queer, two-spirit acronym (LGBTTTQ2), and then discussed the club's aim: "To work toward changing our school to address explicitly sexual orientation, gender identity, gender expression and the questioning of all these things … to include LGBTQ2 material in our school's curriculum." This GSA recommendation follows the lead of Elia (2014) who asserts, "Bisexuality should be thoroughly infused and integrated into the curriculum and not be simply an add-on to existing lesson plans, presentations, or classroom exercises" (p. 47). The GSA members and their advisor were keenly aware of LGBT2Q curricular deficiencies (see Elia, 2014; Kosciw et al., 2014; Taylor et al., 2011) and wanted to make a concerted effort to integrate education about the 'other' in everyday schooling (see Kumashiro, 2002). In sum, student-led professional development workshops, such as the one facilitated by Skylar, are key learning opportunities that can help educators generate a greater understanding of bi/pansexualities (McAllum, 2014).

Teacher versus student understandings: Learning through the internet and GSA participation

It was clear that students' knowledge of sexual diversity and fluidity, including pansexuality, was more sophisticated than their GSA advisors. Contributing factors included online research (see Lapointe, 2015a), and knowledge exchange within GSAs (Lapointe, 2014, 2015b). Skylar asserted:

> It is safe to say that I've gotten most of my sexual education towards LGBTQ communities from [the] internet and the GSA as opposed to getting it in the school system where it should be more mandatory so that people like me [who are pansexual] and people who are transgender don't feel as if they're being selected out and treated differently and poorly.

She went on to say, "I've done my research. So, Tumblr helps … sexuality on Tumblr is the freaking rainbow, every shade of it. You can literally get black too, navy blue, there's everything. It's not black and white. It's beautiful. I love it." With the exception of Azariah, all students relied on social media (e.g., Tumblr, Instagram, etc.) to develop and enhance their SGM knowledge base. Zion also recognized the need to follow students' lead when she stated, "You know I didn't know what pansexual meant. There are so many terms I didn't know myself, so you have to be aware that you're going to have to educate yourself if you don't already know those things." In this humbling passage Zion recognized that self-directed professional development is imperative to her role as an advisor, and that she must play catch-up to GSA members who are more knowledgeable than her in this area. In addition to self-directed learning, Zion also discussed the importance of listening to the perspectives and experiences of youth (see Cook-Sather, 2002).

As Reese stated in their final diary, GSA advisors should be, "Someone who is willing to learn and will not be upset if someone younger than them knows more on a subject than they do." In the following quote Zion described how she learned about bisexuality from Skylar:

> when we first started [the GSA], I think we talked more just about stories. Like I learned about Skylar, umm, you know exploring bisexuality and then you know coming to the conclusion that she's more pansexual…. She gets attracted to a person not a gender or a sex…. I think that's one of the wonderful things about pansexuality … if I could go back and do it all over again I'm not sure that I'd be the same person because I really embrace pansexuality now. And I think that that's true, that it's more allowable to be attracted to a person and not a gender. It's less limiting; it's more loving; it's more free.

This quote demonstrates how GSAs may "help transform the ways in which SGM youth are made intelligible as they challenge the rigidity … of the heterosexual/homosexual and male/female binaries and embrace queerness as a composite of fluid sexual and gender identities.." (Grace & Wells, 2015, p. 283). Through listening to Skylar's identification journey, Zion learned that sexualities can shift throughout time (Britzman, 1995; Ruffolo, 2006). Zion began to appreciate sexual attraction as person specific rather than gender dependent, which enabled her to reimagine her sexuality without the constraints of heteronormative cultural codes and pressures. Advising the GSA opened up queer possibilities in that heteronormativity could be unlearned, making way for new understandings of attraction that problematize the heterosexual matrix (see Butler, 1990). As such, Zion described her newfound understanding of pansexuality as, "It's just … being attracted to the person."

Like Zion, Blake learned about bisexuality through listening to Skylar's self-identification stories. In their second diary Blake wrote:

> I definitely learned a lot about bisexuality, mainly from Skylar. I can shamelessly admit that I was one of those people that thought individuals who identify as bisexual have a preference between males and females, like a "I like girls, but boys are okay, too" kind of thing, but Skylar has so blissfully enlightened me that she very simply likes both boys and girls, and although she may have preferences between certain aspects of males and females, she does not prefer one gender over the other. I understand that not everyone who is bisexual is the same, and some may very well have a preference, but the fact still stands that it doesn't make them any less bisexual because of their preference, and Skylar helped me to understand that.

Similar to Mayo's (2015) assertion that GSAs promote identity reflection, Blake's membership enabled them to reflect deeply on bi/pansexual identities and unlearn harmful biphobic discourses that circulate in school (see Elia, 2010, 2014). Because the wider education system does not encourage learners to interrogate the privileging of heterosexuality and the othering of nonmonosexual identities (see Kumashiro, 2002), the role of GSAs is essential because "all students need to be educated to overcome ignorance, fear, and stereotypes in the work to transgress homo/bi/transphobia and transform schools so they can be SGM-supportive and accommodative spaces" (Grace & Wells, 2015, p. 268).

Most students learned with and from each other through GSA participation (see Lapointe, 2015b), which helped them re/discover queer sexualities and genders that are largely absent in formal education (see Britzman, 1997; Grace & Wells, 2015; Linville, 2009; Miller, 2014). Peyton expressed:

> I had known quite a few things about the LGBT2QIA community, however, this club has definitely expanded my knowledge immensely. I learned more about different orientations and identities such as asexuality, pansexuality and transgender individuals. I have also learned quite a bit about gender fluidity.

Similar to Zion, Peyton advanced her knowledge of the sexuality and gender spectrums (see Britzman, 1995; Grace & Wells, 2015; Ruffolo, 2006) and learned more information about pansexuality in particular. As a result of her participation in the GSA, Taylor also learned more about pansexuality. When asked if she learned anything new Taylor stated:

> Yeah, like the different sexual minorities and different flags. It was kind of like asexual and it's pansexual, and transgender and I can't remember them off the top of my head, but there's a whole bunch of different ones and I kind of had them explained by my friends.

Taylor communicated that when her GSA was developing club shirts students used the Smartboard to Google:

> flags that we could put on it [GSA shirt] because it was in the design, so we looked up the different flags and I was just like, "Hey, what does that mean?" … And then, I followed a

> page on Instagram and it had a whole bunch of different information because I was interested in it and knowing what they were and understanding it more.

This quote demonstrates how GSA activities can not only provide queer/trans education (Lapointe, 2014, 2015a, 2015b; Mayo, 2013) but inspire students to discuss queer topics with their friends and conduct follow-up research. Azariah, Hayden, Peyton, and Taylor's commentary spotlights the educative capacity of GSAs (see Lapointe, 2014, 2015b) and how their traditional role as safe and supportive spaces has been expanded to provide education and awareness (Graybill et al., 2015).

Bi/pansexual integration within GSAs: Room for improvement

Elias (2014) calls for extracurricular clubs, such as GSAs, to include bisexuality in their names because, "Although GSAs support bisexual youth and have been enormously helpful, bisexuality is not sufficiently visible" (p. 47). Besides club names, GSA content should also strive to be more bi/pansexual-inclusive. In fact, a few participants suggested that bi/pan representation was missing in their GSA activities and events. During the fourth observation at Village High Dylan played the video, *Survival of the Fabulous*. The video explored the following questions: "Are gay men actually born gay? If so, what causes this and how could homosexuality have survived the evolutionary process?" (Sage, 2013). While watching the documentary the researcher noted, "What about bisexual people? Pansexual people?" Likewise, in Andie's second diary entry he wrote, "…the video seemed to lack a little connecting to the other sexualities in my opinion." The researcher's and Andie's critiques explore the erasure of nonmonosexual sexualities and the reinstitutionalization of sexual and gender dichotomies in the media. Unfortunately, the documentary was not debriefed afterwards; as such, there was a lost opportunity to problematize the sociocultural privileging of monosexualities (Autumn, 2013; Sears, 2014).

According to Sasha, another opportunity for bi/pansexuality awareness was lost at the GSA assembly. As a part of the GSA's SGM-awareness week the club's advisor, in consultation with GSA members, created a video to show the entire school at the assembly. The theme of the video conveyed the message that every student, staff member, educator, and administrator belonged at school, simply because they go/work there. The video depicted a variety of people quickly describing why they belong at school. For example, in the video people stated, "If you're a drama student you're a [school mascot].' "If you identify as transgender you're a [school mascot]"… "If you're Muslim, you're a [school mascot]." There was a variety of identities that were represented in the short video; but, for Sasha there could have been more pansexual and genderfluid content:

> I would like to have gotten a few more people and a few more, I don't know things said … I don't think we had pansexual in there … because the things you always hear are lesbian, bisexual, gay, trans man, trans woman…. And it's just kind of the idea to get other things

> in there that aren't as heard about, right?... And like pansexuals or people who are genderfluid and stuff like that and just bringing that up

Sasha voiced that pansexuality and other nonmainstream identities are rarely examined at school (see Elia, 2014; McAllum, 2014). Although monosexualities are irrefutably privileged over bi/pansexualities in school (see Elia, 2010, 2014; Roberts et al., 2015), bisexuality and pansexuality were included in the club's video. In the same screen shot, one student stated, "If you're bisexual," then another student stated, "or pansexual," and then they both declared, "you're a [school mascot]." Although bisexuality and pansexuality were mentioned in the video, Sasha did not recall it, perhaps because bi/pansexuality was lost in a sea of non-SGM content. As opposed to its mere inclusion (see Elia, 2014), the intentional and distinct integration of bi/pansexualities within GSA-related events would help educate students about lesser known identities (Lapointe, in press-b), so non-monosexualities may be embraced and celebrated in schools.

Conclusion

This article explored GSA members' and advisor's knowledge of and/or experience with bi/pansexualities. For non-monosexual-identified students, the term 'pansexuality' resonated with their experience of attraction to people rather than genders. More specifically, many students embraced pansexuality to recognize and affirm gender beyond the fe/male binary and to express their potential to be attracted to people regardless of their gender identities. Although bisexuality and pansexuality were characterized as distinct identities, following the findings of Elia (2010, 2014), there was an erasure for nonmonosexualities in formal schooling and GSA activities/events. Similar to Roberts et al.'s (2015) work, bi/panphobic oppression and prejudice was expressed by many people in participants' social networking circles—including SGM GSA members and advisors. Due to hetero/cisnormative social contexts, GSA members felt compelled to learn about SGM content through social media, such as Tumblr and Instagram (see Lapointe, 2015a). Students' nuanced knowledge of sexual diversity and fluidity, as a result of personal experience and online research, calls for educators to engage in SGM-based (self-directed) professional development to match students' understanding. Teachers would be wise to follow the lead of GSA members and incorporate sexual and gender learning, garnered from social media, into their formal curriculum (see Lapointe, 2015a). Besides learning SGM content through online platforms, GSA participation enabled bi/pansexual knowledge exchange among students and teachers, which promoted queer understanding of sexuality and gender that problematized the heterosexual matrix (Butler, 1990; see also Britzman, 1995, 1998). Although GSA involvement facilitated opportunities to discus and unpack preconceived and prejudicial assumptions about bi/pansexualities, it was argued that more concerted efforts should be made within GSAs to integrate educational and affirmative bi/pansexual content. Future research should explore how bi/pansexualities are embraced in GSAs.

References

Autumn, E. (2013). Challenging the binary: Sexual identity that is not duality. *Journal of Bisexuality, 13*(3), 329–337. doi:10.1080/15299716.2013.813421

Britzman, D. (1995). Is there a queer pedagogy? Or, stop reading straight. *Educational Theory, 45*(2), 151–165. doi:10.1111/j.1741-5446.1995.00151.x

Britzman, D. (1997). What is this thing called love? New discourses for understanding gay and lesbian youth. In S. de Castell & M. Bryson (Eds.), *Radical in<ter>ventions: Identity, politics, and difference/s in educational praxis* (pp. 183–207). New York, NY: State University of New York Press.

Britzman, D. (1998). *Lost subjects, contested objects: Towards a psychoanalytic inquiry of learning.* New York, NY: State University of New York Press.

Butler, J. (1990). *Gender trouble: Feminism and the subversion of identity.* New York, NY: Routledge.

Callis, A. S (2014). Bisexual, pansexual, queer: Non-binary identities and the sexual borderlands. *Sexualities, 17*(1/2), 63–80. doi:10.1177/1363460713511094

Carlson, D. (2014). 'It gets better': Queer youth and the history of the "problem of the homosexual" in public education. In S. Ibrahim & S. R. Steinberg (Eds.), *Critical youth studies* (pp. 141–151). New York, NY: Peter Lang Publishing.

Conway, T. R., & Crawford-Fisher, R. (2007). The need for continued research on Gay-Straight-Alliances. *Journal of Curriculum and Pedagogy, 4*(2), 125–129. doi:10.1080/15505170.2007.10411658

Cook-Sather, A. (2002). Authorizing students' perspectives: Toward trust, dialogue, and change in education. *Educational Researcher, 31*(4), 3–14. doi:10.3102/0013189×031004003

Craig, S. L., McInroy, L, McCready, L. T., & Alaggia, R. (2015). Media: A catalyst for resilience in lesbian, gay, bisexual, transgender, and queer youth. *Journal of LGBT Youth, 12*(2), 54–75. doi:10.1080/19361653.2015.1040193

Currie, S., Mayberry, M., & Chenneville, T. (2012). Destabilizing anti-gay environments through Gay-Straight Alliances: Possibilities and limitations through shifting discourses. *The Clearing House: A Journal of Educational Strategies, Issues and Ideas, 85*(2), 56–60. doi:10.1080/00098655.2011.611190

Elia, J. P. (2010). Bisexuality and school culture: School as a prime site for bi-intervention. *Journal of Bisexuality, 10*(4), 452–471. doi:10.1080/15299716.2010.521060

Elia, J. P. (2014). Bisexuality and schooling: Erasure and implications for health, *Journal of Bisexuality, 14*(1), 36–52, doi:10.1080/15299716.2014.872461

Elliott, K. O. (2015). Queering student perspectives: Gender, sexuality and activism in school. *Sex Education: Sexuality, Society and Learning*, 1–14. doi:10.1080/14681811.2015.1051178

Garcia-Alonso, P. M. (2004). *From surviving to thriving: An investigation of the utility of support groups designed to address the special needs of sexual minority youth in public high schools*

(Unpublished doctoral dissertation). Retrieved from Dissertation Abstracts International (UMI Number: 3126026)

Ghaziani, A. (2011). Post-gay collective identity construction. *Social Problems, 58*(1), 99–125. doi:10.1525/sp.2011.58.1.99

Ghaziani, A. (2014). *There goes the gayborhood?* Princeton, NJ: Princeton University Press.

Grace, A. P., & Wells, K. (2015). *Growing into resilience: Sexual and gender minority youth in Canada*. Toronto, Canada: University of Toronto Press.

Graybill, E. C., Varjas, K., Meyers, J., Dever, B. V., Greenberg, D., Roach, A. T., & Morillas, C. (2015). Demographic trends and advocacy experiences of Gay-Straight Alliance Advisors. *Journal of LGBT Youth, 12*(4), 436–461. doi:10.1080/19361653.2015.1077770

Kitchen, J., & Bellini, C. (2013). Making schools safe and inclusive: Gay-Straight Alliances and school climate in Ontario. *Canadian Journal of Educational Administration and Policy, 146*, 1–37.

Kosciw, J. G., Greytak, E. A., Bartkiewicz, M. J., Boesen, M. J., & Palmer, N. A. (2012). *The 2011 national school climate survey: The experiences of lesbian, gay, bisexual and transgender youth in our nation's schools*. New York, NY: Gay, Lesbian, and Straight Education Network (GLSEN).

Kosciw, J. G., Greytak, E. A., Palmer, N. A., & Boesen, M. J. (2014). *The 2013 National School Climate Survey: The experiences of lesbian, gay, bisexual and transgender youth in our nation's schools*. New York, NY: Gay, Lesbian, and Straight Education Network (GLSEN).

Kumashiro, K. (2002). *Troubling education: Queer activism and anti-oppressive pedagogy*. New York, NY: Routledge Falmer.

Lapointe, A. (2014). Gay-Straight Alliance (GSA) members' engagement with sex education in Canadian high schools. *Sex Education: Sexuality, Society and Learning, 14*(6), 707–717. doi:10.1080/14681811.2014.914024

Lapointe, A. (2015a). Queering the social studies: Lessons to be learned from Canadian secondary school Gay-Straight Alliances. *Journal of Social Studies Research*, doi:10.1016/j.jssr.2015.07.004

Lapointe, A. (2015b). Standing 'straight' up to homophobia: Straight allies' involvement in Gay-Straight Alliances (GSA). *Journal of LGBT Youth. 12*(2), 144–169. doi:10.1080/19361653.2014.969867

Lapointe, A. (in press-a). Queering youth studies: Exploring the queer pedagogical insights within the *Critical Youth Studies Reader. Journal of LGBT Youth*, 1–8.

Lapointe, A. (in press-b). Postgay. In E. Brockenbrough, J. Ingrey, W. Martino, & N. M. Rodriguez (Eds.), *Critical concepts in queer studies and education: An international guide for the twenty-first century*. Palgrave Macmillan.

Liboro, R. M., Travers, R., & St. John, A. (2015). Beyond the dialectics and polemics: Canadian Catholic schools addressing LGBT youth issues. *High School Journal, 98*(2), 158–180. doi:10.1353/hsj.2015.0000

Linville, D. (2009). Queer theory and teen sexuality: Unclear lines. In J. Anyon (Ed.), *Theory and educational research: Toward critical social explanation* (pp. 156–174). New York, NY: Routledge.

Mayo, J. B. (2013). Critical pedagogy enacted in the Gay-Straight Alliance: New possibilities for a third space in teacher development. *Educational Researcher, 42*(5), 266–275. doi:10.3102/0013189x13491977

Mayo, J. B. (2015). Youth work in Gay-Straight Alliances: Curriculum, pedagogy, and activist development. *Child & Youth Services, 36*(1), 79–93. doi:10.1080/0145935X.2015.1015887

McAllum, M. (2014). "Bisexuality is just semantics…": Young bisexual women's experiences in New Zealand secondary schools. *Journal of Bisexuality, 14*(1), 75–93. doi:10.1080/15299716.2014.872467

Miceli, M. (2005). *Standing out, standing together: The social and political impact of gay- straight alliances*. New York, NY: Taylor & Francis.

Miller, sj. (2014). Moving an anti-bullying stance into schools: Supporting the identities of transgender and gender variant youth. In S. Ibrahim & S. R. Steinberg (Eds.), *Critical youth studies* (pp. 161–171). New York, NY: Peter Lang Publishing.

Mitchell, R. C., Davis, K. S., & Galupo, M. P. (2015). Comparing perceived experiences of prejudice among self-identified plurisexual individuals. *Psychology & Sexuality*, *6*(3), 245–257. doi:10.1080/19419899.2014.940372

Pallotta-Chiarolli, M. (2010). *Border sexualities, border families in schools*. Lanham, MD: Rowman & Littlefield.

Patton, M. Q. (2002). *Qualitative research & evaluation methods* (3rd ed.). Thousand Oaks, CA: Sage.

Roberts, T. S., Horne, S. G., & Hoyt, W. T. (2015). Between a gay and a straight place: Bisexual individuals' experiences with monosexism, *Journal of Bisexuality*, *15*(4), 554–569, doi:10.1080/15299716.2015.1111183

Ruffolo, D. V. (2006). Queer(ing) scholarly research: Decentering fixed subjects for implicated subjectivities. *Higher Education Perspectives*, *2*(2), Retrieved from: http://hep.oise.utoronto.ca/index.php/hep/article/view/623/679

Russell, S. T., Muraco, A., Subramaniam, A., & Laub, C. (2009). Youth empowerment and school gay-straight alliances. *Journal of Youth and Adolescence*, *38*(7), 891—903. doi:10.1007/s10964-008-9382-8

Rust, P. (2001). Two many and not enough: The meanings of bisexual identities. *Journal of Bisexuality*, *1*(1), 31–68. doi:10.1300/J159v01n01_04

Sage, B. (Writer & Director). (2013). Survival of the fabulous [Documentary series episode]. In D. Suzuki (host), *The nature of things*. Toronto, ON: CBC/Radio Canada.

Saldana, J. (2013). *The coding manual for qualitative researchers*. Thousand Oaks, CA: Sage.

Savin-Williams, R. (2005). *The new gay teenager*. Cambridge, MA: Harvard University Press.

Sears, J. T. (2014) Becoming and being: Bisexuality and the search for self. *Journal of Bisexuality*, *14*(1), 3–6, doi:10.1080/15299716.2014.872447

Sullivan, N. (2003). *A critical introduction to queer theory*. Ney York, NY: New York University Press.

Taylor, C., Peter, T., Campbell, C., Meyer, E., Ristock, J., & Short, D. (2015). *The every teacher project on LGBTQ-inclusive education in Canada's K-12 schools: Final report*. Winnipeg, Canada: Manitoba Teachers' Society.

Taylor, C., Peter, T., McMinn, T. L., Elliott, T., Beldom, S., Ferry, A., ... Schachter, K. (2011). *Every class in every school: The first national climate survey on homophobia, biphobia, and transphobia in Canadian schools*. Toronto, Canada: Egale Canada Human Rights Trust.

Walkley, A. J., & Kinsey, L. M. (2013). *Bi the bi: Does 'bisexual' imply that there are only two genders?* Retrieved from: http://www.huffingtonpost.com/aj-walkley/bisexual-gender-binary_b_2425081.html

Walton, G. (2006). H-cubed: A primer on bullying and sexuality diversity for educators. *Our Schools / Our Selves*, *15*(2), 117–126.

Weiss, J. T. (2003). GL vs. BT: The archaeology of biphobia and transphobia within the US gay and lesbian community. *Journal of Bisexuality*, *3*(3/4), 25–55. doi:10.1300/J159v03n03_02

Wyss, S. E. (2004). 'This was my hell': The violence experience by gender non-conforming youth in US high schools. *International Journal of Qualitative Studies in Education*, *17*(5), 709–730. doi:10.1080/0951839042000253676

Yin, R. K. (2014). *Case study research: Design and methods* (5th ed.). Thousand Oaks, CA: Sage.

"Regardless of Their Gender": Descriptions of Sexual Identity among Bisexual, Pansexual, and Queer Identified Individuals

M. Paz Galupo, Johanna L. Ramirez, and Lex Pulice-Farrow

ABSTRACT

The present research investigates the way individuals under the bisexual umbrella conceptualize their sexual identity. Participants included 172 adults who self-identified as bisexual, pansexual, and queer. Participants individually completed an online survey in which they were asked to describe their sexual identity. Qualitative responses were analyzed via thematic analysis. Four major themes were identified and found relevant to all three identity groups: (1) labeling sexual identity, (2) distinctions of attraction, (3) explicit use of binary/nonbinary language, and (4) identity transcendence. Each of the four major themes was further composed of subthemes, and one minor theme of questioning also emerged. Patterns of responses across sexual identity were analyzed via chi-square analyses. Individuals who self-identified as bisexual, pansexual, and queer demonstrated similarities and differences in the way they described their sexual identities. Of the 15 emergent subthemes, six differed in frequency across sexual identity. Discussion focuses on elucidating when grouping bisexual, pansexual, and queer identities together may prove useful, and when it may further distort an understanding of the range of plurisexual experience.

The present research investigates the way individuals who fall under the bisexual umbrella conceptualize their sexual identity. Specifically, this research takes a comparative approach to understanding the way that individuals who endorse the plurisexual[1] sexual identity labels (i.e., bisexual, pansexual, queer) describe their identities. Understanding similarities and differences across individual meanings of these identity terms can provide a more nuanced understanding of the range of bisexual experience.

Conceptualizing bisexuality and the bisexual umbrella

Contemporary understandings of bisexuality are affected by the way cultural and scientific definitions of 'sexuality' are based upon heteronormative and mononormative assumptions where heterosexual and monosexual experience are considered the natural default (Dean, 2010; Galupo, Davis, Grynkiewicz, & Mitchell, 2014). Sexuality research often explores and defines sexual minority experience in comparison to heterosexual experience. Lesbian, gay, bisexual, and transgender individuals are often grouped under a larger LGBT umbrella, based upon an assumed shared experience of gender nonconformity (Alexander & Yescavage, 2003; Clarke, Hayfield, & Huxley, 2012) and stigma/minority stress (Fassinger & Arseneau, 2007). In addition to the way this LGBT umbrella conflates sexual orientation and gender identity, conceptualizing individuals identifying as LGBT as a unified group can be problematic. For example, individuals identifying as bisexual do not always feel connected to the LGBT community (Balsam & Mohr, 2007; Rust, 1995), experience bi-invisibility or erasure (Nutter-Pridgen, 2015; Yoshino, 2000; Yost & Thomas, 2012), and are subjected to a unique brand of antibisexual prejudice from outside and within the LGBT community (Bostwick & Hequembourg, 2014; Brewster & Moradi, 2010; Israel & Mohr, 2004).

'Bisexuality' is a poorly defined and understudied sexuality in the research literature. When bisexuality is examined, it is often framed in contrast to lesbian and gay experience. Bisexuality, then, is conceptualized as a homogenous middle ground that bridges two monosexual (heterosexual and lesbian/gay) anchors (Galupo, Davis, et al., 2014). Representing bisexuality on a continuum between "same" and "opposite-sex" attraction creates misunderstandings that reinforce a binary conceptualization of bisexuality (Galupo, Lomash, & Mitchell, 2016).

Many individuals identifying as bisexual find current definitions and labels of 'bisexuality' limiting and endorse multiple labels (Mitchell, Davis, & Galupo, 2015; Rust, 2000) or switch labels across different contexts (Belmonte & Holmes, 2016). New labels are being used to counter misconceptualizations about bisexuality and to more accurately define bisexual attraction and experience (Better, 2014). Despite this, scholars have only recently acknowledged other plurisexual identities such as pansexual, fluid, and queer (Callis, 2014; Galupo, Davis, et al., 2014; Galupo, Mitchell, & Davis, 2015; Gonel, 2013; Gray & Desmarais, 2014; Katz-Wise, Reisner, Hughto, & Keo-Meier, 2016; Mitchell, Davis, & Galupo, 2015). More research is needed to capture the range of bisexual experiences and to understand distinctions across plurisexual identities that are often considered under the bisexual umbrella.

Present study

Despite findings that suggest bisexuality is the largest sexual identification group in the LGBT community (e.g., Gates, 2011), little is known about the range of identities often grouped together under the bisexual umbrella. The present study takes an exploratory approach in understanding the way individuals endorsing three of the most common plurisexual identities—bisexual, pansexual, and queer—describe their sexual identities. Thematic analysis was used to characterize emergent themes from participants' qualitative descriptions of their sexual identities. Once themes were identified, each participant's response was coded based on the presence or absence of each theme/subtheme. Chi-square analyses were conducted to examine frequencies of themes across participant self-identification (bisexual, pansexual, queer).

Method

Participant demographics

Participants were 172 adults who self-identified as bisexual ($n = 76$), pansexual ($n = 51$), or queer ($n = 45$). Participants ranged in age from 18 to 77 ($M = 26.18$, $SD = 9.29$). The majority (95.35%) of participants resided in the United States and represented all 50 states and Washington, DC. Table 1 includes participant demographics with regard to racial/ethnic diversity, highest level of education, and socioeconomic status. There was limited racial/ethnic diversity within the sample, with 76.7% identifying as White and 23.3% of participants identifying as a racial/ethnic minority. Demographics did not significantly differ across groups with the exception of age and gender identity (see Table 2).

Recruitment

Recruitment announcements, including a link to the online survey, were posted to social media sites, online message boards, and e-mailed via LGBT listservs. Some of these resources were geared toward specific sexual minority communities

Table 1. Participant demographics.

Plurisexual identity	
Bisexual	44.2%
Pansexual	29.7%
Queer	26.2%
Race/ethnic identity	
American Indian/Alaska Native	0.6%
Asian/Asian American	4.1%
Black/African American	2.3%
Hispanic/Latino	3.5%
Native Hawaiian/Other Pacific Islander	0.6%
White/Caucasian	76.7%
Biracial/Multiracial	5.2%
No Answer	7.0%
Education	
Didn't complete high school or Graduate Equivalency Diploma (GED)	1.8%
High school or GED	12.8%
Some college	46.0%
College	19.7%
Graduate or professional degree	15.7%
Socioeconomic status	
Working class	20.3%
Lower-middle class	15.7%
Middle class	37.8%
Upper-middle class	16.3%
Upper class	0.6%

Table 2. Groups differed across age and gender identity.

	Bisexual $n = 77$	Pansexual $n = 51$	Queer $n = 45$
Mean age (*SD*)	26.80 (10.02)	23.03 (5.95)	27.84 (8.81)
Gender Identity (%)			
Cisgender	89.2	58.8	44.4
Man	21.1	5.9	6.7
Woman	64.5	51.0	26.7
Other	1.3	2.0	11.1
Transgender	10.4	41.2	65.6
Transfeminine	1.3	7.8	0.0
Transmasculine	1.3	5.9	15.5
Gender nonconforming	6.5	19.6	26.6
Agender	0.0	2.0	0.0
Other	1.3	3.9	13.3

including LGBT people of color, whereas others served the plurisexual community more generally. Participants heard about the study primarily through online means, including Facebook (50.0%), Tumblr (15.1%), research-oriented websites/ message boards (15.7%), and receiving a forwarded e-mail from an acquaintance or listserv (4.7%). Other participants were directed to the survey by a friend or significant other (6.4%) and nine participants acquired access to this survey through different venues.

Measures and procedure

The present study focused on information obtained from a demographic section of a larger online study investigating sexual identity and sexual minority experience. A structured sexual orientation question was presented to participants where they chose their primary sexual orientation from discrete options: gay, lesbian, bisexual, pansexual, fluid, queer, asexual, and other. All participants were asked to then list any other sexual identities they endorsed and to respond to the following prompt via free response: "Please describe how you define your sexuality." The present analysis focuses on the responses from participants who self-identified as bisexual, pansexual, and queer.

Data analysis

Using an inductive coding method we sought to identify underlying themes in participants' descriptions of their sexual identity (Braun & Clarke, 2006). Analysis began with all three authors independently coding data looking for themes. All responses in the dataset were analyzed together with participants' grouping (bisexual, pansexual, queer) unknown to the researchers at the time of coding. The research team met and discussed their coding categories and agreed upon an initial set of codes. The second and third author then coded and sorted the data set using the initial set of codes and provided the first author (who served as an external auditor) with a list of themes and sorted quotes based on theme. The entire research team agreed upon the final coding structure and met several additional times to discuss and solidify which quotes would fit under each theme. Final quotes were chosen to simultaneously exemplify each theme and to ensure that the selection of quotes best represented the diversity of bisexual/plurisexual identities endorsed by the sample.

Beyond describing each theme, chi-square analyses were used to highlight patterns of experiences across sexual identity. Four major themes and one minor theme were identified. When including all identified subthemes, 15 different themes/subthemes were coded using a binary (1 = present; 0 = not present) system. Chi-square tests for independence were conducted to examine frequencies of themes across participant self-identification (bisexual, pansexual, queer). For those themes where a significant main effect was found, post-hoc paired comparisons were conducted to further differentiate patterns of responses across groups.

Several checks were included in our data analysis process to increase the credibility of our results. First, at the end of the survey we provided participants with the opportunity to reflect upon how our questions captured (and failed to capture) their individual experiences. Participants were also asked to provide feedback to improve the present and future studies. Some of the responses obtained were incorporated into our analysis as they clarified answers to demographic questions. Second, throughout the data analysis process we discussed the themes and made decisions via consensus. Because of the range of our collective experiences across sexual orientation, gender identity, gender presentation, racial identity, and relationship experiences we came to these discussions with different perspectives. Our research team includes a professor of psychology who self-identifies as a bi/pansexual cisgender woman (first author), a clinical psychology graduate student who identifies as a heterosexual cisgender woman (second author), and a clinical psychology graduate student who identifies as a lesbian/queer genderfluid person (third author).

Results

Our analysis focused on participants' answers to an open-ended question in which they were asked to describe their sexual identity. Four major themes and one minor theme emerged based upon participants' descriptions of their sexual identity. The first had to do with the way identity was described in relation to labels. The second centered on the distinctions participants made when describing their attractions. The third focused on the explicit use of binary/nonbinary language. The fourth focused on the conceptualization of sexual identity in relation to transcendence. A minor theme centered on confusion or questioning of sexual identity. In the sections below we describe each of these themes and their related subthemes. All participant responses can be categorized in at least one of the themes/subthemes and many represent multiple themes, as they are not mutually exclusive.

Table 3. Endorsement of themes among bisexual, pansexual, and queer individuals.

		%			
	Theme	Bisexual	Pansexual	Queer	χ^2
Labels	Multiple labels	10.5	13.7	20.0	2.12
	Explicit lack of label	14.5	13.7	13.3	.034
Distinctions	Preferences: Specifically stated preference of one group over the other	36.8	11.8	33.3	10.12**
	Degree	18.4	3.9	6.7	7.72*
	Partner's identity	13.2	2.0	22.2	9.27*
	Sexual versus romantic attraction	11.8	5.9	2.2	4.04
	Relationships	5.3	2.0	13.3	5.46
	Exclusion criteria	1.3	2.0	8.9	5.32
	Inclusion criteria	3.9	17.6	8.9	6.80*
Binary	Explicit binary	16.9	0	4.6	9.97**
	Explicit nonbinary	19.7	27.4	15.5	2.16
Transcends	Transcends gender/sex	23.7	54.9	15.6	21.73**
	Transcends body	5.3	15.7	8.9	3.94
	Fluidity	11.8	5.9	13.3	1.69
	Confused/questioning	5.9	7.9	4.4	.59

Note. $^{*}p < .05$ $^{**}p < .01$.

We also analyzed patterns that emerged across sexual identity. Table 3 includes the chi-square analyses for each of the 15 subthemes. Individuals who self-identified as bisexual, pansexual, and queer demonstrated similarities and differences in the way they described their sexual identities. Of the 15 emergent themes, six differed in frequency across sexual identity.

"I'm still not 100% sure about labeling myself": Labeling sexual identity

When describing their sexual identity, participants' descriptions often referenced their relationship to labels. Two subthemes emerged in relation to labels: (1) multiple labels and (2) explicit lack of label.

Many participants used multiple labels to describe their identities, as exemplified by the following quotes:

> Sort of a lesbian-leaning kind of bi-romantic grey/demi asexuality. (Queer)
>
> I am bi and queer and pansexual and fluid, all the time, all at once. For the sake of brevity, I usually say either bi or queer. (Bisexual)
>
> Panromantic, polyamorous, and kinky in addition to pansexual. I also feel that being genderqueer, while not a sexuality, does play a role in my love-life. (Pansexual)
>
> Queer or Fluid may be the most accurate terms for my sexual orientation, but bisexual and pansexual labels are more convenient for seeking out communities or social networks. (Queer)

Another way that participants referenced labels in their descriptions was to discuss an explicit lack or rejection of labels. When asked how they describe their sexual identity, participants indicated:

> I don't. I just go with whatever seems to work at the time. (Queer)
>
> I just like people. I'm more attracted to personalities rather than genders. But I'm still not 100% sure about labeling myself. (Pansexual)
>
> I don't try to, usually. It's more a matter of acting freely in company that have no negative feelings towards other orientations. And suppressing my feelings around people that are less accepting. (Bisexual)

Both of these subthemes around labels showed similar patterns across sexual identity (see Table 2); though responses from bisexual, pansexual, and queer individuals expressed these themes, the frequency of expression did not significantly differ across sexual identity.

"I am bisexual, though I prefer men": Distinctions of attraction

In describing their sexual identities participants made salient distinctions among their attractions. With regard to distinctions, seven subthemes emerged: (1) preferences, (2) degree, (3) partner's identity, (4) sexual versus romantic attraction, (5) relationships, (6) exclusion criteria, and (7) inclusion criteria. In general, participants identifying as bisexual (36.8%) and queer (33.3%) were significantly more likely than individuals identifying as pansexual (11.8%), to indicate a stated preference of one group over the other.

Sometimes participants made distinctions in their attraction to different groups of people by labeling the degree of attraction.

> I find myself romantically and physically attracted to both men and women, albeit not equally. I would say that my attraction level is about 65% toward men and 35% toward women. (Bisexual)
>
> I'm queer. I'm in a hetero marriage, but I'm bisexual probably 60% gay 40% straight. (Queer)
>
> I am bisexual, though I prefer men. It's about 70/30. (Bisexual)

As exemplified in the above quotes, even though participants often broke down their attractions to different groups based on percentages or degrees, they did not all group their attractions in the same way. For example, sometimes they were grouped based on gender/sex (as in the first and third quote) and sometimes based on sexual orientation (as in the second quote). Chi-square analyses indicated that individuals identifying as bisexual (18.4%) were more likely than individuals identifying as pansexual (3.9%) or queer (6.7%) to describe their identity based on degree of attraction.

Participants sometimes expressed distinctions in their attraction based on their partner's identity. Individuals identifying as queer (22.2%) and bisexual (13.2%) were significantly more likely than individuals identifying as pansexual (2.0%) to describe their attraction by referencing a preferred identity of partner.

> Femme who primarily dates butches or FTMs, very rare occasional exception of sex with cisgender males or MTFs. (Queer)

> I'm mostly attracted to females or feminine/androgynous people. Whenever I fantasize about masculine men, it feels like it comes from a very feminine side of me. (Pansexual)

> I'm attracted primarily to those who are male-bodied and/or identify as male. I have seriously dated cisgender and transgender men. (Queer)

When describing their attractions, some participants made distinctions between their sexual versus romantic attractions. This theme was expressed similarly across identity (bisexual, pansexual, queer).

> Very bisexual. Tend to be more straight in romantic attachments, and more gay in sexual ones. (Bisexual)

> I am sexually attracted to both men and women but only romantically attracted to women. (Queer)

> I'm very picky about romantic attraction and fairly picky about sexual attraction, too. (Pansexual)

Sometimes participants made salient their relationships when describing their sexual identity. This was similarly expressed across all three identities (bisexual, pansexual, and queer):

> I have had sexual and emotional relationships with both men and women. I ended a heterosexual relationship about eight years ago and am not sure which gender I am more open to now that I am thinking about relationships again. I feel like when I am with a male I'm heterosexual but when I'm with a woman or attracted to a woman I feel lesbian. Bisexual is just a convenient way to label the fact that I have these two orientations. (Bisexual)

> I believe it is clear to mark a distinction between orientation and preference. As someone who identifies as bisexual, I am oriented and attracted towards both sexes, though I prefer to have relationships with men. So, I see orientation as a kind of magnetic compass in which you are oriented towards a certain sex, and then your sexual preferences are those in which you act upon (i.e., pursue relationships with). (Bisexual)

> My definition of my sexual orientation evolves. It is easier to say that I am Pansexual than it is to explain why a Lesbian has a straight male partner and a bisexual female partner, and an occasional transgender partner–without saying that I am Bisexual, or a very confused Lesbian. (Pansexual)

In their descriptions of their sexual identity, participants sometimes indicated who was excluded or included when describing their attraction. For example, the following quotes exemplify the way some participants specified who was excluded from their groups of attraction:

> I am romantically and sexually attracted to all genders and orientations except for cis straight men. (Bisexual)

> I'm attracted to my gender and other genders. I'm not attracted to all genders, therefore not identifying as pansexual. (Bisexual)

I am attracted to people of a number of different genders (though, for what it's worth, rarely those whose gender is identical to my own). (Queer)

Other participants focused on who was included in their attractions:

I like guys and dudes and androgynous people. (Pansexual)

My sexual orientation is fluid. I have a very inclusive definition of bisexuality that isn't restricted to traditional binary gender roles and doesn't exclude trans people (I believe that a ftm trans man is a man, not a separate category). I define my orientation as open to love from multiple genders and able to change. (Bisexual)

I'm mostly attracted to females or feminine/androgynous people. (Pansexual)

I'm a queer male who's sexually aroused by some but not all normatively male-bodied people, and few if any normatively female bodied people. (Queer)

In general, participants were more likely to use inclusion criteria as opposed to exclusion criteria when describing their attractions. In addition, though individuals identifying as bisexual, pansexual, and queer were just as likely to describe their attractions using exclusion criteria, individuals identifying as pansexual (17.6%) and queer (8.9%) were more likely to use inclusion criteria than individuals identifying as bisexual (3.9%).

"My gender and other genders": Explicit use of binary/nonbinary language

A third major theme focused on how participants described their identity in relation to binary/non-binary terms. Two subthemes emerged: (1) explicit binary and (2) explicit non-binary.

Sometimes participants' language referred to gender/sex in dichotomous way, specifically referencing "women and men" or by indicating "two" or "both" genders:

I am attracted to both males and females. (Bisexual)

I refer to myself as a "classic bisexual" I am equally sexually attracted to men and women, and chose a life partner for other traits than what type of genitals they happen to have. (Bisexual)

Individuals identifying as bisexual (16.9%) were more likely than individuals identifying as pansexual (0%) and queer (4.6%) to use binary terminology when describing their own sexual identities. However, a greater number of participants across all three groups (bisexual, pansexual, queer) intentionally used nonbinary language in their descriptions. The use of nonbinary terminology did not differ across group. Nonbinary language was evident where participants explicitly referred to more than cisgender women and men by saying, for example, "all genders," "other genders," or otherwise acknowledging gender diversity.

Attracted to all genders/sexualities as well as those who don't identify with a gender. (Pansexual)

I'm attracted to my gender and other genders. I'm not attracted to all genders, therefore not identifying as pansexual. (Bisexual)

I usually try not to. I'm attracted to people of many different gender identities and presentations–I could easily be perceived as heterosexual in some contexts and as lesbian in others, depending on the perceptions of other people. I choose to define myself as queer when people ask, because it reflects the flexibility I want and allows me to explain further if it is necessary. (Queer)

"Open to love from multiple genders and able to change": Identity transcendence

A third major theme in participants' descriptions of their sexual identity was the concept of transcendence. Subthemes for transcendence included (1) transcends gender/sex, (2) transcends body, and (3) fluidity.

Some participants described their identity as transcending sex and gender. Participants specifically discussed their attraction as transcending the gender/sex of their partner.

I define my sexual orientation by whom I am attracted to and want a romantic relationship with. For me, that is being attracted to a person regardless of their gender. (Bisexual)

It's about loving someone for who they are as a person, not their gender. (Pansexual)

It's more about the particular person than what gender they happen to be. (Queer)

I'm gender-blind. I'll be with a person for who they are, regardless of gender/sex. (Pansexual)

Gender or even sex are inconsequential to my sexual preferences. (Queer)

Although this was a common theme for all three groups, the expression of transcending gender/sex was significantly more frequent among individuals identifying as pansexual (54.9%) when compared to individuals identifying as bisexual (23.7%) and queer (15.6%). In addition, all three groups described their attraction as transcending the body.

I fall in love with the heart not the anatomy. I'm an equal opportunity employer. (Bisexual)

Not being picky about the parts, and only able to be sexually attracted to people if I've gotten to know them well enough to consider them a close friend. (Bisexual)

Interested in people over people's bits. Gender is amongst the many variables that literally do not enter the equation of "to date or not to date. (Pansexual)

I'm interested in people; the bodies are incidental. (Queer)

Participants also described sexual transcendence in their descriptions of their sexuality as fluid. This was seen across individuals identifying as bisexual, pansexual, and queer:

> My sexual orientation is fluid.... I define my orientation as open to love from multiple genders and able to change. (Bisexual)
>
> I define my sexual orientation as very fluid and shifting. (Queer)
>
> Fluid. I love who I love and it seems that that is generally spread across genders. (Bisexual)
>
> This thing that swings around and won't stay still. (Bisexual)
>
> I don't (describe my identity). It changes way too often. (Pansexual)

"Still questioning though": Confusion or sexual identity questioning

A minor theme that was seen across all three groups was the idea that participants were still questioning their sexual identity.

> I go back and forth between bisexual and pansexual because I have not yet really had a chance to completely understand the difference. (Bisexual)
>
> Not completely gay, but leaning more that way than bisexual. Still questioning though. (Queer)

Discussion

The present research focused on descriptions of sexual identity among individuals identifying as bisexual, pansexual, and queer. Participants' descriptions focused on four major themes centered on their (1) relationship to identity labels, (2) distinctions in their attractions, (3) use of binary/nonbinary language, and (4) transcendence of traditional notions of sexuality. These main themes were salient to individuals across all three groups. Overall, there was a great deal of similarity seen across participants' personal definitions and understandings of sexual identity among individuals identifying as bisexual, pansexual, and queer. This was evidenced in the fact that there were no significant differences across groups for nine of the 15 subthemes.

Supporting the notion of a bisexual/plurisexual umbrella

One of the important similarities across the three groups was the way participants described their sexual identity label usage. Although participants did choose a primary sexual identity (forming the basis of their group membership for the study), in their descriptions they often relied on multiple and overlapping labels. This finding is consistent with research that suggests that individuals who endorse plurisexual identities often use multiple labels (Galupo et al., 2015; Gonel, 2013; Rust, 2000). When compared to individuals who endorse monosexual labels, individuals identifying as bisexual/plurisexual are less likely to feel that their sexual identity label fully captures their sexuality (Dyar, Feinstein, & London, 2015) and are more likely to provide additional explanation and context around their labels to fully capture their nonnormative identity (Galupo et al., 2015). Relatedly individuals identifying as bisexual, pansexual, and queer in this study often referenced the way that they explicitly avoid or reject the use of labels. These findings suggest that there are ways that the three sexual identity groupings operate similarly and support the common research practice of grouping these identities together under a larger bisexual/plurisexual umbrella, as it may be appropriate for some research questions.

Binary/nonbinary distinctions

One of the stereotypes of bisexuality (Serano, 2015; Weiss, 2003) and a source of tension in the way bisexuality and pansexuality is often differentiated (Gonel, 2013) is the belief that bisexuality conceptually reinforces the gender binary. For the present study, a major theme that emerged in participants' descriptions of sexual identity centered on the usage of binary and nonbinary language. The present findings indicate that individuals identifying as bisexual are a heterogeneous group and vary with regard to their use of binary/nonbinary terms. Although individuals identifying as bisexual were more likely to use binary language than individuals identifying as pansexual or queer when describing their own attractions, only 16.9% of their responses reflected binary language. In addition, individuals identifying as bisexual used nonbinary terms just as frequently (19.7%) as binary terms and were just as likely to use nonbinary language as their counterparts identifying as pansexual and queer. Taken together, these findings do not support the general misconception that individuals identifying as bisexual define their attractions solely in binary ways, that they rigidly support a binary notion of gender/sex, or that their sexual identity is founded upon the exclusion of individuals identifying as transgender.

Distinctions in identity across bisexual, pansexual, and queer groups

Although there were more similarities than differences, exploring patterns of difference across the three sexual identity groups may provide some guidance regarding the individual meaning ascribed to plurisexual labels. Understanding these differences may suggest areas where collapsing across the three may prove problematic or may conflate the experiences of individuals who endorse bisexual, pansexual, or queer identities.

There were six subthemes where differences were seen (preferences, degree, partner's identity, inclusion criteria, explicit binary, transcends gender/sex). When describing distinctions in their attraction to different groups, participants identifying as bisexual and queer were significantly more likely than individuals identifying as pansexual to state a preference for one group over another, and to indicate a preferred identity for their partner. Individuals identifying as bisexual when compared to individuals identifying as pansexual and queer were also more likely to describe their attractions to different groups based on degree, and to use language that explicitly referred to gender/sex in binary terms. Individuals identifying as pansexual were most likely to describe their attractions by indicating who is included and to describe their identity as transcending gender/sex.

It is important to note that of the six subthemes where differences were found, differences were consistently found between individuals identifying as bisexual and pansexual. Responses of individuals identifying as queer, however, sometimes aligned with individuals identifying as bisexual and sometimes with individuals identifying as pansexual. Like individuals identifying as bisexual, individuals identifying as queer were more likely to state preferences in their attraction, make distinctions in their attraction based on partner identity, and they were also less likely than pansexual individuals to describe their identity as transcending gender/sex. Similar to individuals identifying as pansexual, individuals identifying as queer were less likely to describe their attraction based on degrees, were more likely to endorse inclusion criteria, and were less likely than individuals identifying as bisexual to describe their identity using language that is explicitly binary.

These patterns indicate that individuals who endorse queer identities were distinct from bisexual and pansexual individuals in important ways and may suggest ways that the queer label maps uniquely onto attraction. Although some researchers have explored queer alongside bisexual and pansexual identities or under a bisexual/plurisexual umbrella (e.g., Callis, 2014; Galupo, Mitchell, Grynkiewicz, & Davis, 2014; Rust, 2000), this grouping has been met with mixed results (Galupo et al., 2015). 'Queer' as a label has a unique history within the larger LGBT community and has been used by some individuals as an umbrella label for the entire community (inclusive of monosexual/plurisexual identities) and by some individuals who have monosexual attractions (Gray & Desmarais, 2014), suggesting that queer may not be easily incorporated into sexual orientation distinctions based on monosexual/plurisexual conceptualizations (Galupo et al., 2015).

Limitations and demographic considerations

A limitation of the present research is that our participants represent a convenience sample collected online. Online recruitment is particularly useful for sexual minority research where participants may have concerns regarding privacy and may not otherwise have access to participate (Riggle, Rostosky, & Reedy, 2005). This may be particularly true for individuals who endorse plurisexual identities as they may be less connected to off-line resources for sexual minority individuals due to antibisexual prejudice from within the larger LGBT community (Brewster & Moradi, 2010). Our sample demographics, however, are consistent with online sampling that over-represents White, middle-class, and educated individuals (Dillman, Smyth, & Christian, 2008). Thus, the present findings should be interpreted within the context of these sample demographics.

The present research illustrated similarities and differences among individuals who primarily endorsed bisexual, pansexual, and queer identity labels. Although participants did self-select into these groups there is the possibility that asking them to select a "primary identity" may have skewed the results toward finding differences, as distinctions among the three groups may not always be salient to the participants. For example, between 10%–20% of the participants endorsed multiple labels and some of the participants' qualitative responses suggested that they equally used the three different labels or that they shift which term they used across different social contexts.

Although important similarities and differences were seen across the three sexual identity groups, it is important to note that two participant demographics also varied across these three primary sexual identity groupings. Participants who endorsed a pansexual identity in this study were significantly younger ($M = 23.0$) than those who endorsed bisexual ($M = 26.8$) or queer ($M = 27.8$) identities. This finding is consistent with the fact that pansexual and queer terms have more recently emerged as common labels within the LGBT community (Callis, 2014; Elizabeth, 2013; Gonel, 2013). In addition, individuals identifying as queer (65.6%) and pansexual (41.2%) were more likely to identify as transgender or indicate a transgender history or status than were individuals identifying as bisexual (10.4%). This supports research that has shown that it is common for individuals identifying as transgender to endorse plurisexual labels (Dargie, Blair, Pukall, & Coyle, 2014; Galupo, Henise, & Mercer, 2016: Kuper, Nussbaum, & Mustanski, 2012). Future research should also consider the ways that gender diversity within the transgender community is related to sexual identity labels (Galupo, Henise, & Mercer, 2016) and experience of sexual fluidity (Katz-Wise et al., 2016). These findings support the recent suggestions that gender diversity should be taken into account when measuring sexual orientation (Galupo, Davis, et al, 2014; Galupo, Lomash, & Mitchell, 2016), conceptualizing sexual identity (Galupo, Henise, & Mercer, 2016; Tate, 2012), and should be fully incorporated into general theories of sexuality (van Anders, 2015).

Conclusion

The present study offers a direct comparison in the way individuals identifying as bisexual, pansexual, and queer conceptualize their sexual identity. Important similarities were found across the three identity groupings supporting the notion that there are meaningful ways in which these identities operate similarly under the 'bisexual umbrella.' Importantly, the present findings suggested that individuals who endorse a bisexual label are just as likely as those who endorse a pansexual and queer label to describe their identity using nonbinary terminology. This finding runs counter to the stereotype that bisexual individuals uniformly adhere to a binary conceptualization of sex and gender. Another similarity across the three groups was that way that individuals identifying as bisexual, pansexual, and queer related to the usage of sexual identity labels. All three described using multiple labels and, at times, preferring no label. These findings support the idea that for some research questions it may be appropriate to group these identity groups together.

Despite the similarities, however, there were some areas where the three groups differed. Of the 15 emergent themes, differences across the groups were found for six themes. For these six themes, differences were consistently found between individuals identifying as bisexual and pansexual. Responses of participants identifying as queer, however, were distinct and sometimes aligned with participants identifying as bisexual and sometimes with participants identifying as pansexual. Researchers should carefully consider the way that individuals identifying as bisexual, pansexual, and queer conceptualize their sexual identity in relation to the topic under study and explore whether the grouping conventions they adopt may skew their findings if differences are ignored.

Funding

This research was supported in part by a grant from the American Institute of Bisexuality awarded to the first author.

Note

1. We use 'plurisexual' to refer to identities that are not explicitly based on attraction to one sex and leave open the potential for attraction to more than one sex/gender; e.g., bisexual, pansexual, queer, and fluid. The term 'plurisexual' is used instead of nonmonosexual because it does not linguistically assume monosexual as the ideal conceptualization of sexuality (see Galupo, Davis, Grynkiewicz, & Mitchell, 2014).

References

Alexander, J., & Yescavage, K. (2003). Bisexuality and transgenderism. *Journal of Bisexuality, 3* (3/4), 1–23. doi:10.1300/J159v03n03_01

Balsam, K. F., & Mohr, J. J. (2007). Adaptation to sexual orientation stigma: A comparison of bisexual and lesbian/gay adults. *Journal of Counseling Psychology, 54*(3), 306–319.

Belmonte, K., & Holmes, T. R. (2016). Outside the LGBTQ "safety zone": Lesbian and bisexual women negotiate sexual identity across multiple ecological contexts. *Journal of Bisexuality, 16*(2), 233–269. doi:10.1080/15299716.2016.1152932

Better, A. (2014). Redefining queer: Women's relationships and identity in an age of sexual fluidity. *Sexuality & Culture, 18*, 16–38. doi:10.1007/s12119-013-9171-8

Bostwick, W. B., & Hequembourg, A. (2014). 'Just a little hint': Bisexual-specific microaggressions and their connection to epistemic injustices. *Culture, Health & Sexuality, 16*(5), 488–503. doi:10.1080/13691058.2014.889754

Braun, V., & Clarke, V. (2006). Using thematic analysis in psychology. *Qualitative Research in Psychology, 3*, 77–101. doi:10.1191/1478088706qp063oa

Brewster, M. E., & Moradi, B. (2010). Perceived experiences of anti-bisexual prejudice: Instrument development and evaluation. *Journal of Counseling Psychology, 57*, 451–468. doi:10.1037/a0021116

Callis, A. S. (2014). Bisexual, pansexual, queer: Non-binary identities and the sexual borderlands. *Sexualities, 17*, 63–80. doi:10.1177/1363460713511094

Clarke, V., Hayfield, N., & Huxley, C. (2012). Lesbian, gay, bisexual and trans appearance and embodiment: A critical review of the psychological literature. *Psychology of Sexualities Review, 3*(1), 51–70. ISSN 2047-1467 Retrieved from http://eprints.uwe.ac.uk/17812

Dargie, E., Blair, K., Pukall, C., & Coyle, S. (2014). Somewhere under the rainbow: Exploring the identities and experiences of trans persons. *Canadian Journal of Human Sexuality, 23*(2), 69–74. doi:10.3138/cjhs.2378

Dean, J. J. (2010). Thinking intersectionality: Sexualities and the politics of multiple identities. In Y. Taylor, S. Hines, & M. Casey (Eds.), *Theorizing intersectionality and sexuality* (pp. 119–139). New York, NY: Palgrave Macmillan.

Dillman, D., Smyth, J., & Christian, L. M. (2008). *Internet, mail, and mixed-mode surveys: The tailored design method.* New York, NY: Wiley.

Dyar, C., Feinstein, B. A., & London, B. (2015). Mediators of differences between lesbians and bisexual women in sexual identity and minority stress. *Psychology of Sexual Orientation and Gender Diversity, 2*(1), 43–51. doi:10.1037/sg0000090

Elizabeth, A. (2013). Challenging the binary: Sexual identity that is not duality. *Journal of Bisexuality, 13*, 329–337. doi:10.1080/15299716.2013.813421

Fassinger, R. E., & Arseneau, J. R. (2007). "I'd rather get wet than be under the umbrella": Differentiating the experiences and identities of lesbian, gay, bisexual, and transgender people. In K. J. Biesche, R. M. Perez, & K. A. DeBord (Eds.), *Handbook of counseling and psychotherapy with lesbian, gay, bisexual, and transgender clients* (pp. 19–49). Washington, DC: American Psychological Association.

Galupo, M. P., Davis, K. S., Grynkiewicz, A., & Mitchell, R. C. (2014). Conceptualization of sexual orientation identity among sexual minorities: Patterns across sexual and gender identity. *Journal of Bisexuality, 14*(3/4), 433–456. doi:10.1080/15299716.2014.933466

Galupo, M. P., Henise, S. B., & Mercer, N. L. (2016). "The labels don't work very well": Transgender individuals' conceptualizations of sexual orientation and sexual identity. *International Journal of Transgenderism, 17*, 1–12. doi:10.1080/15532739.2016.1189373

Galupo, M. P., Lomash, E., & Mitchell, R. C. (2016). "All of my lovers fit into this scale": Sexual minority individuals' responses to two novel measures of sexual orientation. *Journal of Homosexuality*, doi:10.1080/00918369.2016.1174027

Galupo, M. P., Mitchell, R. C., & Davis, K. S. (2015). Sexual minority self-identification: Multiple identities and complexity. *Psychology of Sexual Orientation and Gender Diversity, 2*, 355–364. doi:10.1037/sgd0000131

Galupo, M. P., Mitchell, R. C., Grynkiewicz, A. L., & Davis, K. S. (2014). Sexual minority reflections on the Kinsey Scale and the Klein Sexual Orientation Grid: Conceptualization and Measurement. *Journal of Bisexuality, 14*, 404–432. doi:10.1080/15299716.2014.929553

Gates, G. J. (2011). *How many people are lesbian, gay, bisexual, and transgender?* Retrieved from http://williamsinstitute.law.ucla.edu/wp-content/uploads/Gates-How-Many-People-LGBT-Apr-2011.pdf

Gonel, A. H. (2013). Pansexual identification in online communities: Employing a collaborative queer method to study pansexuality. *Graduate Journal of Social Science, 10*(1), 36–59.

Gray, A., & Demarais, S. (2014). Not all one and the same: Sexual identity, activism, and collective self-esteem. *Canadian Journal of Human Sexuality, 23*(3), 116–122. doi:10.3138/cjhs.2400

Israel, T., & Mohr, J. J. (2004). Attitudes toward bisexual women and men. *Journal of Bisexuality, 4*(1/2), 117–134. doi:10.1300/J159v04n01_09

Katz-Wise, S., Reisner, S. L., Hughto, J. W., & Keo-Meier, C. L. (2016). Differences in sexual orientation diversity and sexual fluidity in attractions among gender minority adults in Massachusetts. *Journal of Sex Research, 53*(1), 74–84. doi:10.1080/00224499.2014.1003028

Kuper, L. E., Nussbaum, R., & Mustanski, B. (2012). Exploring the diversity of gender and sexual orientation identities in an online sample of transgender individuals. *Journal of Sex Research, 49*, 244–254. doi:10.1080/00224499.2011.596954

Mitchell, R. C., Davis, K. S., & Galupo, M. P. (2015). Comparing perceived experiences of sexual prejudice among plurisexual individuals. *Psychology & Sexuality, 6*(3), 245–257. doi:10.1080/19419899.2014.940372

Nutter-Pridgen, K. L. (2015). The old, the new, and the redefined: Identifying the discourses in contemporary bisexual activism. *Journal of Bisexuality, 15*, 385–413. doi:10.1080/15299716.2015.1033044

Riggle, E. D. B., Rostosky, S. S., & Reedy, C. S. (2005). Online surveys for BGLT research. *Journal of Homosexuality, 49*, 1–21. doi:10.1300/J082v49n01-01

Rust, P. C. (1995). *Bisexuality and the challenge to lesbian politics: Sex, loyalty, and revolution.* New York, NY: New York University Press.

Rust, P. C. (2000). Two many and not enough: The meaning of bisexual identities. *Journal of Bisexuality, 1*, 31–68. doi:10.1300/J159v01n01_04

Serano, J. (2013). *Excluded: Making feminist and queer movements more inclusive.* Berkeley, CA: Seal Press.

Tate, C. C. (2012). Considering lesbian identity from a social-psychological perspective: Two different models of "being a lesbian". *Journal of Lesbian Studies, 16*(1), 17–29. doi:10.1080/10894160.2011.557639

van Anders, S. M. (2015). Beyond sexual orientation: Integrating gender/sex and diverse sexualities in sexual configurations theory. *Archives of Sexual Behavior, 44*(5), 1177–1213. doi:10.1007/s10508-015-0490-8

Weiss, J. T. (2003). GL vs. BT: The archaeology of biphobia and transphobia in the U.S. lesbian and gay community. *Journal of Bisexuality, 3*, 25–55. doi:10.1300/J159v03n03_02

Yoshino, K. (2000). The epistemic contract of bisexual erasure. *Stanford Law Review, 52*, 353–461. Retrieved from http://www.kenjiyoshino.com/articles/epistemiccontract.pdf

Yost, M. R., & Thomas, G. D. (2012). Gender and binegativity: Men's and women's attitudes toward male and female bisexuals. *Archives of Sexual Behavior, 41*(3), 691–702.

We're Here and We're Queer: Sexual Orientation and Sexual Fluidity Differences Between Bisexual and Queer Women

Ethan H. Mereish, Sabra L. Katz-Wise, and Julie Woulfe

ABSTRACT

Theorists and researchers have noted an overlap between individuals who are bisexually-identified and queer-identified. Although early definitions of bisexuality may have been predominantly binary (i.e., attracted to women and men), in recent years there has been a move toward a more "queer" understanding of bisexuality (e.g., attraction to more than one gender beyond women and men). The purpose of this study was to examine similarities and differences between adult women who were bisexually-identified and those who were queer-identified, ages 18 to 66 years, on sociodemographic characteristics, two dimensions of sexual orientation (sexual behaviors and attractions), fluidity in attractions and sexual orientation identity, and identity centrality and affirmation in an online sample (N = 489), which was mostly from the United States (73.5%). Results indicated that women who are bisexual and queer were similar in terms of sociodemographic characteristics, with the exception of education; women identifying as queer were more educated than women identifying as bisexual. Women identifying as queer were also more likely than women identifying as bisexual to report variability in their sexual behaviors and attractions and more fluidity in their sexual orientation identity. Additionally, women identifying as queer reported higher levels of identity centrality and affirmation than women identifying as bisexual. Considerations for sexual minority women's health research are discussed.

Greater attention to experiences of women identifying as bisexual is warranted, given their elevated health risks and the large focus on women identifying as lesbian as compared to women identifying as bisexual in the literature (Barker et al., 2012). The emerging body of literature on women identifying as bisexual suggests that they experience distinct forms of oppression (Brewster & Moradi, 2010; Dyar, Feinstein, & London, 2014; Eliason, 1997; Israel & Mohr, 2004; Mohr & Rochlen, 1999) and fare worse than women identifying as lesbian on several physical and mental health metrics including cardiovascular disease risk (Conron, Mimiaga, & Landers, 2010; Dilley, Simmons, Boysun, Pizacani, & Stark, 2010), anxiety (Jorm, Korten, Rodgers, Jacomb, & Christensen, 2002; Kerr, Santurri, & Peters, 2013), depression (Jorm et al., 2002; Kerr et al., 2013; Pyra et al., 2014), suicidality (Conron et al., 2010; Pompili et al., 2014), and violence and victimization (Breiding, Chen, & Black, 2010). These disparities highlight the need for more investigation into the unique experiences of women identifying as bisexual.

'Bisexuality' varies greatly in how it is defined and measured. Some definitions include some degree of same-sex attraction, same-sex feelings, or sexual behavior over the course of the lifetime, whereas other definitions propose that 'bisexuality' refers only to individuals who self-identify as bisexual (Meyer & Wilson, 2009). Similarly, individuals identifying as bisexual may differ in their own definitions of and meanings associated with bisexuality (Rust, 2000, 2002). Identifying as bisexual may have different political and social meanings, including an engagement with gender politics, increasing bisexual visibility within a context of biphobia and invisibility, and connection with other individuals or communities identifying as bisexual (Rust, 2000). Individuals identifying as bisexual may also use more than one sexual orientation identity label (Rust, 2000). In particular, many individuals also identify with a "queer" identity label. One survey of participants at a bisexual conference indicated that 54% of the attendees identified as queer and bisexual (Barker, Bowes-Catton, Iantaffi, Cassidy, & Brewer, 2008).

'Queer,' a term used in the beginning of the 20th century to mean "odd" or "strange," was originally applied derogatively to sexual minorities (Barker, Richards, & Bowes-Catton, 2009). In recent years, the use of 'queer' as an identity label has been reclaimed by gender and sexual minorities (Drechsler, 2003). For example, queer theory within an academic context emerged as the critical analysis of fixed binary categories of identity—gender and sexuality specifically, and notions of the self more broadly. Further, given that queer theory challenges fixed notions of identity, queer has also become an umbrella term for gender and sexual minorities (Barker et al., 2009; Drechsler, 2003).

Theorists and researchers alike have noted an overlap between individuals who identify as queer and those who identify as bisexual. Whereas early definitions of 'bisexuality' may have been predominantly binary (i.e., attracted to women and men), in recent years there has been a move toward a more "queer" understanding of bisexuality (e.g., attraction to more than one gender beyond female and male; Barker et al., 2009; Drechsler, 2003). In addition, many women identifying as bisexual have adopted a queer identity label (Barker et al., 2008). This raises important questions for researchers. For example, do women identifying as bisexual and queer share similar sociodemographic features? Differences may exist in sociodemographic characteristics such as education, as many individuals may learn about the term 'queer' in college courses. What are the distinctions between women identifying as bisexual and queer in their patterns of sexual behaviors, attractions, and identity? It is possible that women identifying as queer are more likely than women identifying as bisexual to have attractions toward individuals who are transgender (identifying with a different gender from one's sex assigned at birth), because queer identity more easily encompasses attraction to more than two genders. Are there differences between women identifying as bisexual and queer in how they understand their sexual orientation identity? Specifically, do women identifying as bisexual and queer differ in the degree to which their sexual orientation identity is central to their overall identity (i.e., identity centrality)? Similarly, how similar or different are the two groups in the degree to which they positively consider and affirm their sexual orientation identities (i.e., identity affirmation)? The use of 'queer identity' may be a form of resistance in response to more conventional sexual orientation identity labels, perhaps making it more central to overall identity than bisexual identity. Alternately, bisexual identity is often stigmatized or erased. Those who choose to embrace the bisexual label may also be acting in resistance to this stigma, making bisexual identity more central and visible. Further research could offer insight into these dimensions for each respective identity.

Given the lack of attention to the distinctions between women identifying as bisexual and queer in research, the purpose of this study was to provide an initial investigation of these questions by analyzing the similarities and differences between a sample of adult women identifying as either bisexual or queer on sociodemographic characteristics, two dimensions of sexual orientation (sexual behaviors and attractions), sexual fluidity in attractions and sexual orientation identity, and sexual orientation identity centrality and affirmation. Examining similarities and differences between women identifying as bisexual and queer may help shed knowledge on what is "under the bisexual umbrella."

Method

Participants

Participants were 489 adult women, ages 18 to 66 years ($M = 28.42$, $SD = 9.66$), from a larger sample of bisexual adults. Participants whose data were included in the current analysis identified their gender as female/woman and their sexual orientation as bisexual (82.4%) or queer (17.6%). Participants who identified their gender as male/man or as transgender were excluded from this analysis because they did not select the female/woman response option. Participants who identified as lesbian ($n = 7$), gay ($n = 2$), heterosexual ($n = 5$), don't know ($n = 6$), unsure/questioning ($n = 15$), or other ($n = 40$) were also excluded because there were too few participants to conduct comparisons among these groups. Overall, the sample of participants was primarily White (81.6%). The participants varied greatly in terms of education, income, employment, geographic location, and relationship status. See Table 1 for sociodemographic information.

Table 1. Sample demographics ($N = 489$).

	Sexual Orientation		
	Bisexual $n = 403$	Queer $n = 86$	Test Statistic
	M (*SD*)	*M* (*SD*)	
Age	28.36 (10.00)	28.30 (8.15)	$F(1, 444) = .002$
	% (*n*)	% (*n*)	χ^2(df)
Race/ethnicity			$\chi^2(7) = 5.48$
Asian/Pacific Islander	1.5 (6)	2.3 (2)	$p = .73$
Black or African American	2.5 (10)	2.3 (2)	
Hispanic/Latina/o	5.5 (22)	2.3 (2)	
White (non-Hispanic)	81.3 (327)	82.6 (71)	
Biracial or multiracial	7.5 (30)	7.0 (6)	
Other	1.7 (7)	3.5 (3)	
Education			χ^2 $(2) = 7.65$
High school degree/Graduate Equivalency Diploma or less	37.5 (151)	26.7 (23)	$p = .02$
College degree	36.2 (146)	32.6 (28)	
Graduate degree	26.3 (106)	40.7 (35)	
Employment			$\chi^2(4) = 7.96$
Full-time	34.7 (140)	32.6 (28)	$p = .09$
Part-time	9.9 (40)	14.0 (12)	
Student	39.2 (158)	47.7 (41)	
Unemployed	10.2 (41)	4.7 (4)	
Other	6.0 (24)	1.2 (1)	
Individual Income			χ^2 $(5) = 1.41$
≤ $9,999	42.9 (169)	38.4 (33)	$p = .92$
$10,000 – $19,999	14.2 (56)	14.0 (12)	
$20,000 – $29,999	13.7 (54)	15.1 (13)	
$30,000 – $49,999	12.9 (51)	14.0 (12)	
$50,000 – $69,999	8.9 (35)	8.1 (7)	
≥ $70,000	7.4 (29)	10.5 (9)	
Geographical region			$\chi^2(7) = 10.27$
Northeastern United States	19.7 (79)	32.6 (28)	$p = .17$
Midwestern United States	15.5 (62)	18.6 (16)	
Northwestern United States	4.7 (19)	5.8 (5)	
Southern United States	12.5 (50)	7.0 (6)	
Southwestern United States	7.0 (28)	5.8 (5)	
Western United States	13.0 (52)	8.1 (7)	
Other U.S. territory	0.2 (1)	0.0 (0)	
International/non-U.S. territory	27.4 (110)	22.1 (19)	
Relationship status			$\chi^2(4) = 6.16$
Single	39.2 (158)	30.2 (26)	$p = .19$
Dating	10.9 (44)	11.6 (10)	
Partnered/committed relationship	30.5 (123)	41.9 (36)	
Married	18.4 (74)	14.0 (12)	
Separated/divorced	1.0 (4)	2.3 (2)	

Note. Participants who racially identified as "other" provided responses such as Native American, Middle Eastern, Armenian, or Jewish. Participants who identified as "other" for employment provided responses such as "stay-at-home parent," "homemaker," and "disabled".

Procedures

An online sample of bisexual women were recruited as part of a larger survey on bisexuality and health. Participants were recruited using a web-based sampling procedure by contacting bisexual-specific online groups and listservs. Internet recruitment of participants has been identified as a successful and common method to obtain broader and more representative samples (Kraut et al., 2004) and to reach sexual minority populations that have been previously overlooked

(Meyer & Wilson, 2009). Inclusion criteria were being 18 years of age or older, and identifying as bisexual and/or having attractions to more than one gender. All potential participants received a link to the data collection website, on which they provided informed consent, completed an online survey, and had the option of being entered into a raffle for monetary incentives for their participation. At the end of the survey, participants were presented with a list of online resources providing lesbian, gay, bisexual, transgender, queer (LGBTQ)-specific mental health support and services. The study was approved by the researchers' Institutional Review Board. The data were cleaned and screened for missingness. Of the participants in this study, some had missing data on the item level; however, no item had more than 0.4% item-level missingness, with the exception of the fluidity in attraction and identity questions, which had missingness of 14.8% and 15.8%, respectively. Participants with missing data for those two questions were excluded only for analyses specific to these two variables.

Measures

Sociodemographic information

Participants completed a basic demographic questionnaire in which they provided information on their age, gender, racial/ethnic background, sexual orientation, highest level of completed education, current employment status, gross annual income, current geographic location, and current relationship status. Participants were permitted to select only one response option for each sociodemographic measure, including gender and sexual orientation label measures. The specific categories for each variable are presented in Table 1.

Dimensions of sexual orientation

Participants completed measures assessing behavioral and attraction dimensions of their sexual orientation, as described below.

Sexual behaviors. Participants were asked with whom they had sex during the past year and over their lifetime with the following two questions created for this study: "During the past year, with whom have you had sex?" and "With whom have you had sex in your lifetime?" Response options were men only; women only; transgender and/or genderqueer individuals only; men and women only; men, women, transgender, and/or genderqueer individuals; and did not have sex during the past year/did not have sex in lifetime.

Sexual attraction. Participants described to whom they were attracted, using an item adapted from the National National Center for Health Statistics, Centers for Disease Control and Prevention (2002): "People are different in their sexual attraction to other people. Which best describes your feelings? Are you:" and were provided with the following response options: only attracted to men or transmen, mostly attracted to men or transmen, equally attracted to men/transmen and women/transwomen, mostly attracted to women or transwomen, only attracted to women or transwomen, not sure, and other.

Sexual fluidity

Participants completed measures assessing sexual fluidity in attractions and identity, as described below.

Fluidity in attractions. We used the Sexual Fluidity Scale (Katz-Wise, 2014) to assess lifetime fluidity in participants' attractions. Participants were asked "Have you ever experienced a change in attractions to others? (For example, feeling only attracted to women, then feeling attracted to both women and men)" and, if they answered *yes* to this item, they were asked: "Have you experienced more than one change in attractions?" Response options were *yes* or *no*.

Fluidity in sexual orientation identity. In addition to assessing fluidity in attractions, we also assessed fluidity in sexual orientation identity using the Sexual Fluidity Scale (Katz-Wise, 2014). Participants were asked, "Have you ever experienced a change in your sexual identity (the labels you use to describe your sexual orientation)?" and, if they answered *yes* to this item, they were asked: "Have you experienced more than one change in your sexual identity?" Response options were *yes* or *no*.

Sexual orientation identity

Participants completed measures assessing two additional aspects of their identity, as described below.

Identity centrality. We used the 5-item identity centrality subscale of the Lesbian, Gay, and Bisexual Identity Scale (LGBIS; Mohr & Kendra, 2011) to assess participants' view of their sexual orientation identity as central to their overall identity. Sample items are "My sexual orientation is a central part of my identity" and "Being an LGB [lesbian, gay, bisexual] person is a very important aspect of my life." Item response options are on a 6-point rating scale from 1 (*disagree strongly*) to 6 (*agree strongly*). For this study, Cronbach alpha reliability was 0.84.

Identity affirmation. We used the 3-item identity affirmation subscale of the LGBIS (Mohr & Kendra, 2011) to assess participants' affirmation of their sexual orientation identity. The three items are: "I am glad to be an LGB person," "I'm proud to be part of the LGB community," and "I am proud to be LGB." Item response options are on a 6-point rating scale from 1 (*disagree strongly*) to 6 (*agree strongly*). For this study, Cronbach alpha reliability was 0.89.

Results

We conducted a 2-group (bisexual vs. queer) ANOVA to test for group differences in age and bivariate analyses to test for group differences in other sociodemographic characteristics. Results from the bivariate analyses indicated that women identifying as queer reported a significantly higher education level than women identifying as bisexual (Table 1). There were no other significant sociodemographic differences.

We conducted bivariate analyses to test for group differences between women identifying as either bisexual or queer in behavioral and attraction dimensions of sexual orientation, and in fluidity of attractions and sexual orientation identity. We used chi-square tests followed by z-tests for variables that included more than four cells (i.e., sexual behaviors and sexual attractions). As reported in Table 2, there were significant differences in sexual behaviors and attractions, and in fluidity of sexual orientation identity; there were no significant differences in fluidity of attractions. In terms of the sexual behavior dimension of sexual orientation, women identifying as queer were more likely than women identifying as bisexual to have had sex with men, women, and transgender and/or genderqueer individuals in the past year and over their lifetime. Women identifying as bisexual were more likely than women identifying as queer to report no sexual partners in the past year and over their lifetime and were more likely to have had sex with men and women only in their lifetime. Women identifying as queer were also more likely than women identifying as bisexual to have had sex with transgender and/or genderqueer individuals only in the past year and lifetime; however, these are not robust findings given the small cell sizes for these comparisons.

In terms of the sexual attraction dimension of sexual orientation, women identifying as bisexual were more likely than women identifying as queer to report equal attraction to men/transmen and women/transwomen, whereas women identifying as queer were more likely than women identifying as bisexual to report attraction to one gender more than the other as well as attraction to "other." Finally, in terms of sexual fluidity, women identifying as queer were significantly more likely than women identifying as bisexual to report having ever experienced a change in sexual orientation identity and to report experiencing more than one change. No significant differences were found in fluidity of attractions.

We conducted 2-group (bisexual vs. queer) Analysis of covariance (ANCOVAs) to test for group differences between women identifying as either bisexual or queer in identity centrality and affirmation, while controlling for education. There were significant differences for both aspects of identity (Table 2). While accounting for education, women identifying as queer reported higher levels of identity centrality and identity affirmation than women identifying as bisexual, these effects were in the moderate range (Cohen's $d = .50$ for centrality and $d = .38$ for affirmation).

Table 2. Descriptive statistics for sexual orientation dimensions ($N = 489$).

	Sexual Orientation		
	Bisexual $n = 403$ % (n)	Queer $n = 86$ % (n)	Test Statistic χ^2 (df)
Sexual behavior dimension			
Past year sex partners			$\chi^2(5) = 56.58$, $p < .000$
Men only	35.7 (144)	26.7 (23)	
Women only	8.4 (34)	11.6 (10)	
Transgender and/or genderqueer individuals only	0.5 (2)	10.5 (9)	B < Q
Men and women only	19.6 (79)	16.3 (14)	
Men, women, transgender, and/or genderqueer	4.5 (18)	17.4 (15)	B < Q
Did not have sex during the past year	31.3 (126)	17.4 (15)	Q < B
Lifetime sex partners			$\chi^2(6) = 41.38$, $p < .000$
Men only	13.4 (54)	7.0 (6)	
Women only	3.0 (12)	3.5 (3)	
Transgender and/or genderqueer individuals only	0.0 (0)	2.3 (3)	B < Q
Men and women only	48.4 (195)	34.9 (30)	Q < B
Men, women, transgender, and/or genderqueer	17.4 (70)	43.0 (37)	B < Q
Did not have sex in lifetime	17.6 (71)	8.1 (7)	Q < B
Sexual attraction dimension			
Attraction			$\chi^2(5) = 25.16$, $p < .000$
Only attracted to men or transmen	0.2 (1)	0.0 (0)	
Mostly attracted to men or transmen	15.1 (61)	23.3 (20)	
Equally attracted to men/transmen and women/transwomen	55.1 (222)	32.6 (28)	Q < B
Mostly attracted to women or transwomen	16.6 (67)	26.7 (23)	B < Q
Only attracted to women or transwomen	0.0 (0)	0.0 (0)	
Not sure	6.2 (25)	1.2 (1)	
Other			
Sexual fluidity in attractions	6.7 (27)	16.3 (14)	B < Q
Ever experienced a change in attraction to others			$\chi^2(1) = 2.51$
Yes	59.8 (222)	70.4 (57)	
No	40.2 (149)	29.6 (24)	
Ever experienced more than one change in attractions			$\chi^2(1) = 2.51$
Yes	62.4 (138)	73.7 (42)	
No	37.6 (83)	26.3 (15)	
Sexual fluidity in sexual orientation identity			
Ever experienced a change in sexual identity			$\chi^2(1) = 16.90$, $p < .000$
Yes	67.0 (248)	90.0 (72)	
No	33.0 (122)	10.0 (8)	
Ever experienced more than one change in sexual identity			$\chi^2(1) = 14.12$, $p < .000$
Yes	39.5 (94)	64.8 (46)	
No	60.5 (144)	35.2 (25)	
	M (SD)	M (SD)	F(df)
Identity centrality	4.23 (0.98)	4.88 (0.89)	$F(1, 357) = 24.45$, $p < .000$, $d = .50$
Identity affirmation	4.78 (1.0)	5.25 (0.75)	$F(1, 375) = 12.55$, $p < .000$, $d = .38$

Note. B = bisexual; Q = queer.
Participants who selected "other" for the attraction category reported several responses, including: "it varies over time," "attracted to all genders," and "depends on person".

Discussion

The aim of this study was to describe similarities and differences in sexual orientation dimensions, sexual fluidity, and identity centrality and affirmation between adult women identifying as either bisexual or queer in a sample of individuals who either identified as bisexual or had attractions to more than one gender. The two groups were remarkably similar in terms of sociodemographic characteristics, with the exception of education; women identifying as queer reported a higher level of education than bisexual women. This may be a reflection of the origins of 'queer' as an identity label emerging out of academic writing. Those with greater education may have more exposure to the theoretical underpinnings of the term 'queer' (e.g., in college or university courses), and in turn may be more likely to adopt this as an identity.

In contrast to sociodemographic characteristics, other findings related to sexual orientation and sexual fluidity revealed numerous significant differences between women identifying as queer compared to women identifying as bisexual. Women identifying as queer were more likely to have had sex with transgender and/or genderqueer individuals, whereas women identifying as bisexual were more likely to report no sexual partners. Greater likelihood of transgender and/or genderqueer sex partners among women identifying as queer may be related to conventional definitions of 'bisexuality' that reflect a binary understanding of gender that may not include individuals identifying as transgender (Barker et al., 2008; Drechsler, 2003). Queer identification is common among gender minority (i.e., transgender and gender nonconfoming) individuals (Katz-Wise, Reisner, Hughto, & Keo-Meier, 2016; Kuper, Nussbaum, & Mustanski, 2011; Meier, Pardo, Labuski, & Babcock, 2013), in part because of the complexity of describing sexual orientation in this population. Similarly, women with transgender and/or genderqueer sexual partners may feel that the queer label best describes their experiences (Joslin-Roher & Wheeler, 2009).

Significant differences between queer and bisexual women were also found for sexual attraction. Women identifying as bisexual were more likely to report equal attraction to men/transmen and women/transwomen, whereas women identifying as queer were more likely to report being mostly attracted to one gender or "other" genders. Women identifying as queer who experience more attraction to one gender may feel that their experiences are not captured within conventional definitions of 'bisexuality' as reflecting equal attraction to women and men. Although researchers have begun to explore the multiple ways in which the queer label is used, particularly within bisexual communities (Barker et al., 2009), more research is needed to better understand why individuals choose to label their sexual orientation as queer and what this label means to them.

Interestingly, no significant difference was found between women identifying as queer or bisexual regarding sexual fluidity in attractions. Previous research has indicated that women who report sexual fluidity in attractions are more likely to identify with identities that reflect attraction toward more than one gender, such as bisexual or queer (Katz-Wise, 2014), in part because the label of queer may allow for greater sexual fluidity (Barker et al., 2009). However, women identifying as queer were significantly more likely than women identifying as bisexual to report having ever experienced a change in sexual orientation identity and to report experiencing more than one change. This may be related to developmental timing of exposure to the term 'queer.' For instance, a woman may identify as bisexual in high school and then identify as queer in college after learning about this identity. This may also occur in relation to a partner's gender transition (i.e., social and/or medical steps taken to align a transgender person's body with their gender identity), which in turn may lead to changes in an individual's orientation label (Joslin-Roher & Wheeler, 2009).

Differences between women identifying as queer or bisexual were also found in measures of identity centrality and affirmation, with women identifying as queer reporting higher levels of both aspects of identity. Identity centrality represents the importance of persons' identity to their overall identity, whereas identity affirmation represents positive thoughts and feelings linked to a person's LGB identity (Mohr & Kendra, 2011). This finding suggests that identifying as queer may be a more positive experience than identifying as bisexual, in terms of women's sense of self. Previous research has found LGB identity affirmation to be negatively associated with depression and sadness, and positively associated with satisfaction with life and self-esteem (Mohr & Kendra, 2011). These associations may also be true for women identifying as queer, though to our knowledge, this has not yet been studied. Having high levels of identity centrality and affirmation may also be protective for women identifying as queer by giving them greater access to community support and resources than bisexual women. Moreover, differences in identity centrality and affirmation may be related to experiences of biphobia. Identifying as queer is related to variability in sexual attractions, including either exclusive same-sex attractions or attractions to more than one gender; thus, women identifying as queer may experience less biphobia than women identifying as bisexual. Thus, increased experiences of biphobia among women identifying as bisexual may be related to lower identity centrality and affirmation compared to women identifying as queer. Future research is needed to better understand these relationships.

A number of limitations should be mentioned. Use of an online sampling design may have excluded sections of the population who have less access to computers (e.g., individuals of low socioeconomic status) or are less likely to use the Internet (e.g., older adults). In addition, the primarily White race/ethnicity of the sample limits generalizability to other races/ethnicities. Future research could use targeted sampling to obtain a more diverse sample in terms of socioeconomic status and race/ethnicity. Moreover, almost one half of the sample identified as being a student. However, the mean age of our sample was higher than traditionally aged college students; thus, our sample captured diverse developmental periods beyond the traditional college years.

There were also limitations in our gender and sexual identity label response options, and our sexual behavior response options. With regard to gender, participants who identified their gender as male/man or as transgender were excluded from this analysis because they did not identify as a female/woman. Given that we did not assess sex assigned at birth, it is unclear whether our sample is solely comprised of cisgender women or whether it also included transgender women. It is important to note that people identifying as transgender and other gender minorities may also identify as queer or bisexual; thus, future research is needed to better understand their experiences. Our sexual orientation identity measure was similarly limited because we did not provide participants the option to choose more than one identity label (e.g., identifying as bisexual *and* queer). There may be overlap between the experiences of these groups that is not captured by examining them as dichotomous. This study is also limited because we did not assess other sexual orientation labels in the bisexuality spectrum, such as sexually fluid and pansexual. Our options for the gender of one's sexual partners in the past year also did not allow participants to select multiple options. Future research would benefit from offering participants broader response options to better capture their behaviors and self-identification.

Findings from the current study have numerous implications for research on the health of women identifying as bisexual and queer. We found that women identifying as queer were more likely than women identifying as bisexual to report having sexual partners who are transgender and/or genderqueer. This may indicate that cisgender (i.e., identifying with the gender that aligns with one's sex assigned at birth) women identifying as queer are more likely than cisgender women identifying as bisexual to be exposed to secondary gender-minority stress based on their status as partners of transgender individuals. Experiencing this type of stress could negatively affect their health. Previous research has also found a link between sexual fluidity of sexual orientation identity and negative health behaviors and outcomes, including substance use (Ott et al., 2013), obesity (Katz-Wise et al., 2014), and depression (Everett, 2015). Greater fluidity of sexual orientation identity among women identifying as queer compared to women identifying as bisexual may put women identifying as queer at greater risk for negative health outcomes. However, the majority of studies of bisexuality and health have not included "queer" as a response option for sexual orientation identity questions, which have not allowed researchers to examine links between sexual fluidity and health among women identifying as bisexual versus women identifying as queer.

Previous research has also suggested that the more central a person's LGB identity is to their overall identity, the more they may be affected by minority stress (Meyer, 2003). The finding that women identifying as queer have greater identity centrality than women identifying as bisexual may translate into more negative health effects of minority stress on women identifying as queer compared to women identifying as bisexual. However, little research has examined health among women identifying as queer. Women identifying as bisexual have worse health outcomes than heterosexual and other sexual minority women and men (Balsam, Beauchaine, Mickey, & Rothblum, 2005; Bauer, Flanders, MacLeod, & Ross, 2016; Case et al., 2004; Conron et al., 2010; Dodge, Sandfort, & Firestein, 2007; Lehavot, 2012), especially those who self-identify with the bisexual label only as compared to the combination of bisexual and other sexual minority labels (Bauer et al., 2016); thus, more research is needed to understand these health disparities among women identifying as bisexual and women identifying as queer.

We offer a number of recommendations based on findings from the current study. First, research on bisexuality should utilize sampling and recruitment strategies that are inclusive of all individuals who fall within the bisexual spectrum—including those who identify as queer. Specifically, studies should recruit participants based on bisexual identity and attraction to and/or sexual behavior with more than one gender, as in Ebin's (2012) definition of 'bisexual health.' Second, measures assessing sexual orientation identity should include "queer" as a response option. Third, individuals identifying as queer should be analyzed separately from individuals identifying as bisexual whenever possible. This could yield important information regarding differences in identity and health between queer and heterosexual individuals and between women identifying as queer individuals and other sexual minorities.

In conclusion, although women identifying as either queer or bisexual in the current study demonstrated similarities on most sociodemographic characteristics, they demonstrated differences in a number of aspects of sexual orientation dimensions, sexual fluidity, and identity centrality and affirmation, suggesting that women identifying as queer are a unique subgroup of women within the spectrum of bisexuality with variability in their sexual behaviors and attractions and fluidity in their sexual orientation identity. Rather than considering queer and bisexual identities as equivalent or entirely independent, future research on identity and health of women identifying as bisexual must consider these as related but distinct identities and examine them independently to better understand their unique health risks and resilience. Considering the experiences of women identifying as queer is an important step toward shedding light on the diversity of experiences among all sexual minority women.

Funding

Dr. Mereish was supported in part by the National Institute on Drug Abuse (T32DA016184) and Dr. Katz-Wise was supported by a grant from the Eunice Kennedy Shriver National Institute of Child Health and Human Development (K99HD082340).

References

Balsam, K. F., Beauchaine, T. P., Mickey, R. M., & Rothblum, E. D. (2005). Mental health of lesbian, gay, bisexual, and heterosexual siblings: Effects of gender, sexual orientation, and family. *Journal of Abnormal Psychology, 114*(3), 471–476. doi:10.1037/0021-843X.114.3.471

Barker, M., Bowes-Catton, H., Iantaffi, A., Cassidy, A., & Brewer, L. (2008). British bisexuality: A snapshot of bisexual representations and identities in the United Kingdom. *Journal of Bisexuality, 8*(1/2), 141–162. doi:10.1080/15299710802143026

Barker, M., Richards, C., & Bowes-Catton, H. (2009). "All the world is queer save thee and me…": Defining queer and bi at a critical sexology seminar. *Journal of Bisexuality, 9*(3/4), 363–379. doi:10.1080/15299710903316638

Barker, M., Yockney, J., Richards, C., Jones, R., Bowes-Catton, H., & Plowman, T. (2012). Guidelines for researching and writing about bisexuality. *Journal of Bisexuality, 12*(3), 376–392. doi:10.1080/15299716.2012.702618

Bauer, G. R., Flanders, C., MacLeod, M. A., & Ross, L. E. (2016). Occurrence of multiple mental health or substance use outcomes among bisexuals: A respondent-driven sampling study. *BMC Public Health, 16*(1), 1–11. doi:10.1186/s12889-016-3173-z

Breiding, M. J., Chen, J., & Black, M. C. (2010). Intimate Partner Violence in the United States—2010. Atlanta, GA: National Center for Injury Prevention and Control, Centers for Disease Control and Prevention.

Brewster, M. E., & Moradi, B. (2010). Perceived experiences of anti-bisexual prejudice: Instrument development and evaluation. *Journal of Counseling Psychology, 57*(4), 451–468. doi:10.1037/a0021116

Case, P., Austin, S. B., Hunter, D. J., Manson, J. E., Malspeis, S., Willett, W. C., & Spiegelman, D. (2004). Sexual orientation, health risk factors, and physical functioning in the Nurses' Health Study II. *Journal of Women's Health, 13*, 1033–1047. doi:doi:10.1089/jwh.2004.13.1033

Conron, K. J., Mimiaga, M. J., & Landers, S. J. (2010). A population-based study of sexual orientation identity and gender differences in adult health. *American Journal of Public Health, 100*(10), 1953–1960. doi:10.2105/AJPH.2009.174169

Dilley, J. A., Simmons, K. W., Boysun, M. J., Pizacani, B. A., & Stark, M. J. (2010). Demonstrating the importance and feasibility of including sexual orientation in public health surveys: Health disparities in the Pacific Northwest. *American Journal of Public Health, 100*(3), 460–467. doi:10.2105/AJPH.2007.130336

Dodge, B., & Sandfort, T. G. (2007). A review of mental health research on bisexual individuals when compared to homosexual and heterosexual individuals. In B. A. Firestein (Ed.), Becoming visible: Counseling bisexuals across the lifespan (pp. 28–51). New York: Columbia University Press.

Drechsler, C. (2003). We are all others. *Journal of Bisexuality, 3*(3/4), 265–275. doi:10.1300/J159v03n03_18

Dyar, C., Feinstein, B. A., & London, B. (2014). Dimensions of sexual identity and minority stress among bisexual women: The role of partner gender. *Psychology of Sexual Orientation and Gender Diversity, 1*(4), 441–451. doi:10.1037/sgd0000063

Ebin, J. (2012). Why bisexual health? *Journal of Bisexuality, 12*(2), 168–177. doi:10.1080/15299716.2012.674854

Eliason, M. (1997). The prevalence and nature of biphobia in heterosexual undergraduate students. *Archives of Sexual Behavior, 26*(3), 317–326. doi:10.1023/A:1024527032040

Everett, B. (2015). Sexual orientation identity change and depressive symptoms: A longitudinal analysis. *Journal of Health and Social Behavior, 56*(1), 37–58. doi:10.1177/0022146514568349

Israel, T., & Mohr, J. J. (2004). Attitudes toward bisexual women and men. *Journal of Bisexuality, 4*(1/2), 117–134. doi:10.1300/J159v04n01_09

Jorm, A. F., Korten, A. E., Rodgers, B., Jacomb, P. A., & Christensen, H. (2002). Sexual orientation and mental health: Results from a community survey of young and middle-aged adults. *British Journal of Psychiatry, 180*(5), 423–427. doi:10.1192/bjp.180.5.423

Joslin-Roher, E., & Wheeler, D. P. (2009). Partners in transition: The transition experience of lesbian, bisexual, and queer identified partners of transgender men. *Journal of Gay & Lesbian Social Services, 21*(1), 30–48. doi:10.1080/10538720802494743

Katz-Wise, S. L. (2014). Sexual fluidity in young adult women and men: Associations with sexual orientation and sexual identity development. *Psychology & Sexuality, 6*, 1–20. doi:10.1080/19419899.2013.876445

Katz-Wise, S. L., Jun, H.-J., Corliss, H. L., Jackson, B., Haines, J., & Austin, S. B. (2014). Child abuse as a predictor of gendered sexual orientation disparities in body mass index trajectories among U.S. youth from the Growing Up Today Study. *Journal of Adolescent Health, 54*(6), 730–738. doi:http://dx.doi.org/10.1016/j.jadohealth.2013.11.006

Katz-Wise, S. L., Reisner, S. L., Hughto, J. W., & Keo-Meier, C. L. (2016). Differences in sexual orientation diversity and sexual fluidity in attractions among gender minority adults in Massachusetts. *Journal of Sex Research, 53*(1), 74–84. doi:10.1080/00224499.2014.1003028

Kerr, D. L., Santurri, L., & Peters, P. (2013). A comparison of lesbian, bisexual, and heterosexual college undergraduate women on selected mental health issues. *Journal of American College Health, 61*(4), 185–194. doi:10.1080/07448481.2013.787619

Kraut, R., Olson, J., Banaji, M., Bruckman, A., Cohen, J., & Couper, M. (2004). Psychological research online: Report of Board of Scientific Affairs' Advisory Group on the conduct of research on the Internet. *American Psychologist, 59*(2), 105–117. doi:10.1037/0003-066X.59.2.105

Kuper, L. E., Nussbaum, R., & Mustanski, B. (2011). Exploring the diversity of gender and sexual orientation identities in an online sample of transgender individuals. *Journal of Sex Research, 49*(2/3), 244–254. doi:10.1080/00224499.2011.596954

Lehavot, K. (2012). Coping strategies and health in a national sample of sexual minority women. *American Journal of Orthopsychiatry, 82*(4), 494–504. doi:10.1111/j.1939-0025.2012.01178.x

Meier, S. C., Pardo, S., Labuski, C., & Babcock, J. (2013). Measures of clinical health among female-to-male transgender persons as a function of sexual orientation. *Archives of Sexual Behavior, 42*(3), 463–474. doi:10.1007/s10508-012-0052-2

Meyer, I. H. (2003). Prejudice, social stress, and mental health in lesbian, gay, and bisexual populations: Conceptual issues and research evidence. *Psychological Bulletin, 129*(5), 674–697. doi:10.1037/0033-2909.129.5.674

Meyer, I. H., & Wilson, P. A. (2009). Sampling lesbian, gay, and bisexual populations. *Journal of Counseling Psychology, 56*(1), 23–31. doi:10.1037/a0014587

Mohr, J. J., & Kendra, M. S. (2011). Revision and extension of a multidimensional measure of sexual minority identity: The Lesbian, Gay, and Bisexual Identity Scale. *Journal of Counseling Psychology, 58*(2), 234–245. doi:10.1037/a0022858

Mohr, J. J., & Rochlen, A. B. (1999). Measuring attitudes regarding bisexuality in lesbian, gay male, and heterosexual populations. *Journal of Counseling Psychology, 46*(3), 353–369. doi:10.1037/0022-0167.46.3.353

National Center for Health Statistics, Centers for Disease Control and Prevention. (2002). National Survey of Family Growth 2002. Atlanta, GA.

Ott, M. Q., Wypij, D., Corliss, H. L., Rosario, M., Reisner, S. L., Gordon, A. R., & Austin, S. B. (2013). Repeated changes in reported sexual orientation identity linked to substance use behaviors in youth. *Journal of Adolescent Health, 52*(4), 465–472. doi:10.1016/j.jadohealth.2012.08.004

Pompili, M., Lester, D., Forte, A., Seretti, M. E., Erbuto, D., Lamis, D. A., … Girardi, P. (2014). Bisexuality and suicide: A systematic review of the current literature. *Journal of Sexual Medicine, 11*(8), 1903–1913. doi:10.1111/jsm.12581

Pyra, M., Weber, K. M., Wilson, T. E., Cohen, J., Murchison, L., Goparaju, L., … Cohen, M. H. (2014). Sexual minority women and depressive symptoms throughout adulthood. *American Journal of Public Health, 104*(12), e83–e90. doi:10.2105/AJPH.2014.302259

Rust, P. C. (2000). Two many and not enough. *Journal of Bisexuality, 1*(1), 31–68. doi:10.1300/J159v01n01_04

Rust, P. C. (2002). Bisexuality: The state of the union. *Annual Review of Sex Research, 13*(1), 180–240.

Index